MW00694764

COVERING POLITICS IN THE AGE OF TRUMP

COVERING POLITICS IN THE AGE OF TRUMP

EDITED BY JERRY CEPPOS

LOUISIANA STATE UNIVERSITY PRESS

BATON ROUGE

Published with the assistance of LSU's Manship School of Mass Communication

Published by Louisiana State University Press
www.lsupress.org

Copyright © 2021 by Louisiana State University Press
All rights reserved. Except in the case of brief quotations used in articles or reviews, no part of this publication may be reproduced or transmitted in any format or by any means without written permission of Louisiana State University Press.

Designer: Michelle A. Neustrom
Typeface: Minion Pro

Cover photograph courtesy the White House and photographer D. Myles Cullen

Library of Congress Cataloging-in-Publication Data

Names: Ceppos, Jerry, editor.
Title: Covering politics in the age of Trump / edited by Jerry Ceppos.
Description: Baton Rouge : Louisiana State University Press, 2021. |
    Includes index.
Identifiers: LCCN 2020050683 (print) | LCCN 2020050684 (ebook) | ISBN
    978-0-8071-7573-6 (paperback) | ISBN 978-0-8071-7595-8 (pdf) | ISBN
    978-0-8071-7596-5 (epub)
Subjects: LCSH: Trump, Donald, 1946—Press coverage. | Presidents—Press
    coverage—United States—History—21st century. | United
    States—Politics and government—2017—Press coverage. | Press and
    politics—United States—History—21st century. | Journalism—Political
    aspects—United States—History—21st century.
Classification: LCC E912 .C68 2021 (print) | LCC E912 (ebook) | DDC
    973.933092—dc23
LC record available at https://lccn.loc.gov/2020050683
LC ebook record available at https://lccn.loc.gov/2020050684

To Dean Martin Johnson
teacher, scholar, leader, colleague, friend

CONTENTS

PREFACE

MARTIN JOHNSON, dean of Louisiana State University's Manship School of Mass Communication, called me in December 2019 with an idea: What would I think of editing a collection of essays by Washington journalists about their experiences covering President Trump and his administration?

The idea was vintage Martin, tailored for me even though we never had talked about a book. Martin knew the interests of every faculty member—and many of our hundreds of students—because he spent so much of his time chatting with us. He knew that I was fascinated by the relationship of the Trump administration with the media—and that I was fortunate enough to know many top Washington journalists because of my fifty years in journalism.

Ten months later, during the week that this manuscript went to the publisher, Martin died in his sleep at age fifty. I hope that he would approve of the execution of his idea.

THE IRONY OF THE 2020 campaign was that journalism dominated a campaign run by the most journalism-averse president of modern times. The first presidential debate was dominated by news generated by enterprising journalists—the exposé by the *New York Times* about Trump's taxes, the explosive tapes recorded by Bob Woodward about the president's knowledge of the pandemic, and others. "It's just fake news," President Trump said at the debate, as he has for years. Hours before the debate, Tim Murtaugh, director of communications for the Trump campaign, complained about "the hostile Washington press corps."

Because of the fraught relationship, we invited some of our essayists to write about their own relationships with President Trump. As a rule, journalists don't like writing about themselves. However, we asked some of our essayists to put that convention aside because the media's relationship with President Trump has been a peculiarly adversarial one.

In fact, five journalists in this collection write about being singled out angrily by President Trump for criticism. "The president's public hostility toward individual reporters was unprecedented," the veteran Washington journalist Clark Hoyt writes.

But the hostility often wasn't a private message. President Trump made his disdain for the media known to all. No modern president "ever has spoken like this about a free and independent press," Major Garrett of CBS News explains. We hope that these essays offer an insight into how journalists continued to report objectively—even though the Trump administration's hostility grew with time.

As we were putting this book together, the coronavirus paralyzed the United States. One of the journalists we consulted, who has covered Washington for more than fifty years, told me that "the virus is consonant with the greater-than-ever hostility (beyond tension) between Trump and the press. . . . This is a highly dangerous situation and can cost lives. There's never been anything like this before." Many others also cited the danger of the situation.

Journalist and scholar Tom Rosenstiel found that none of this happened by mistake: "When he calls news 'fake,' it is a signal telling people to disbelieve any source but him. When he calls the press 'the enemy of the people,' he implies that any criticism of him really is a criticism of them for supporting him. And when he calls a news organization 'failing,' as he frequently described the *New York Times,* the underlying message is that the traditional media and their approach to fact-based independent reporting are on the wrong side of history—that his authoritarian view of reality, the leader as the sole source of truth and belief over facts as the best guide to knowledge, is the way of the future."

That's why we asked twenty-four of the nation's top journalists, almost all of them covering the White House or politics in general, why the relationship has become so difficult. We asked practitioners, young and old, from every medium and background. (We also asked the White House to weigh in but never received a reply.)

I'm glad we asked so many because each has a different take. For example, four of our authors write that the media themselves bear part of the blame. As Charlie Cook, of the *Cook Political Report*, told me, "It's the lack of awareness of many journalists that is so frustrating. They don't seem to understand that they are playing into their enemies' and skeptics' narratives."

Others point out that this was not the first president to tussle with the media. The first was George Washington, as Harold Holzer notes in *The Presidents vs. the Press: The Endless Battle between the White House and the Media*.

"Nearly all presidents, from Washington to Trump, have reacted to press criticism in this manner: treating what we now call 'the media' as the enemy," Holzer writes. He notes that Trump's critics say he tries to circumvent established media by using new platforms, "but so did Washington, Jefferson, Jackson, Theodore Roosevelt, and Lyndon B. Johnson."

THANKS TO THE Society of Professional Journalists Foundation for supporting this project philanthropically. SPJ has been a part of my life since college, so its confidence in this project is special to me. Thanks to all of the essayists, who taught me about life in the trenches, which is so much more difficult than in my thirty-six years in newsrooms. Thanks, too, to graduate assistant Kyle Stanley for his help. This book also would not be possible without my funding from William B. Dickinson Professorship.

And thank you most to my wife, Karen. When Martin called with the idea for this book, she had just finished nursing me back to health over the course of five months after a "minor" surgery went wrong. This book certainly would not exist without her. Nor would I.

I HOPE THIS BOOK reminds us that the media and the president should have an adversarial relationship—but not one that makes covering Trump "a massive earthquake," as Mark Leibovich of the *New York Times* calls it in his essay: "It is scary and feels dangerous, and the full extent of the carnage to the world as we knew it will not be understood for years. Grave damage has been done to institutions, to norms and certainly to the way people view journalists and consume journalism."

—Jerry Ceppos

JERRY CEPPOS has worked in journalism and journalism education for more than fifty years. He is the former executive editor of the *San Jose Mercury News* and former vice president for news of Knight Ridder, at the time the second-largest US newspaper publisher. He is the former dean of the Reynolds School of Journalism at the University of Nevada, Reno, and of Louisiana State University's Manship School of Mass Communication. He now is the William B. Dickinson Distinguished Professor at the Manship School. He was a winner of the first Ethics in Journalism Award granted by the Society of Professional Journalists. He also is a Fellow of SPJ, the highest professional honor given by the society, "for extraordinary contribution to the profession." He is a former president of the Associated Press Managing Editors, a national group, and served two terms as president of the Accrediting Council on Education in Journalism and Mass Communications, which sets standards for journalism and mass-communication schools and measures whether they achieve those standards. He is a "distinguished journalism alumnus" of the University of Maryland.

COVERING POLITICS
IN THE AGE OF
TRUMP

I

WHEN THE PRESIDENT CALLS YOU OUT

WHEN WE ASKED top political journalists to write about their experiences covering President Trump, we had no idea that four of them would write about being criticized rudely and publicly (and one would write about being criticized privately). Most chilling was the experience of McKay Coppins of *The Atlantic*: "He denounced me on Twitter as a 'slimebag reporter' and 'true garbage with no credibility.' He got me blacklisted from political events where he was speaking. His secretary sent an addendum to the $850 bill for my stay at Mar-a-Lago, claiming they had forgotten to include the cost of the flight: $10,000. I even received a cryptic note late one night from a Republican opposition researcher, who told me someone had tried to hire him to investigate my personal life."

Rebecca Buck of CNN, Ashley Parker of the *Washington Post,* and Jill Colvin of the Associated Press also make clear that it's no fun to be called out by the president during fervid Trump rallies. And Mark Leibovich of the *New York Times* writes that even a private dressing-down can be memorable.

REVISITING A FATEFUL TRIP TO MAR-A-LAGO

MCKAY COPPINS

IT DIDN'T FEEL at the time like a story I would be telling for the rest of my life. It was January of 2014, and I had traveled to New Hampshire to see Donald Trump, the host of *Celebrity Apprentice,* deliver a speech about his supposed political aspirations. No one took him seriously, of course. Trump had been pulling this particular publicity stunt for decades, flirting with a presidential bid every time he had a book to sell or a TV show to promote. The schtick long ago had worn thin, especially with the press. When I'd e-mailed my editors at BuzzFeed News to pitch them on a Trump story, I practically could hear the weary sighs through my inbox. *Fine,* the response came back, *but please don't waste too much time on this.*

My plan was simple: Interview Trump on the flight back to New York aboard his private jet, extract a handful of blustery quotes, and file a brief, colorful story about a celebrity billionaire playing at politics. Not my most important journalistic contribution, perhaps, but worth a day's work.

Once Trump finished his speech, I squeezed into the back of his black SUV and we rolled through the frozen streets of Manchester toward the airstrip where his plane was waiting. A few minutes before we arrived, however, his pilot called to report that a blizzard was shutting down LaGuardia Airport. Trump called an audible: Why not skip New York and fly straight on to Palm Beach, home to his famous oceanside compound, Mar-a-Lago?

As schedules were reorganized and flight plans rerouted, one of Trump's aides reminded him that they had a reporter in tow, and inquired as to what should be done with me. "Bring him to Florida!" the future president replied—and, before I had time to process what was happening,

3

I was strapped into a creamy leather seat on Trump's 757, eating pretzels as we soared southward.

I spent two surreal days at Trump's Xanadu, during which he seemed determined to impress me. He bragged about how much better his plane was than the charter jet Mitt Romney had used for his presidential campaign. ("Total piece of shit.") He bragged about how enlightened he was. ("I am so not a racist, it's incredible.") He even bragged about the beauty of Mar-a-Lago's female patrons. ("There are a lot of good-looking women here," he told me, leaning in as he adopted a low-pitched purr.)

But, in retrospect, there was one moment when I should have paid closer attention. We were sitting in his den, a giant Trump portrait hanging on the walnut-paneled wall above us, as he riffed on his philosophy of media combat. Trump, who had spent his career seducing and sparring with the New York City tabloids, described the role of journalism in fundamentally transactional terms. When the stories about him were nice, the journalists were to be rewarded; when they were not, they were to be punished. (Truth and accuracy were lesser concerns.)

"If I am treated unfairly," he told me, "I will go after that reporter."

"Are you going to come after me when this article comes out?" I asked, mostly joking.

"Maybe."

By the time I returned home to New York, I had formed an impression of Trump as an almost tragic figure—insecure, unhappy, and thirsty for affirmation. As I wrote in what ended up being a 6,000-word profile, Trump struck me as "startled by his suddenly fading relevance and consumed by a desperate need to get it back." Rereading the story years later, this portrait of Trump has held up reasonably well, I think. Less prescient was my confident prediction that Trump was "about as likely to run for president in his lifetime as he is to accept follicular defeat." When the story was published in February, it carried the headline, "36 Hours On the Fake Campaign Trail With Donald Trump."

Trump, infuriated, spent the next several weeks lashing out. He denounced me on Twitter as a "slimebag reporter" and "true garbage with no credibility." He got me blacklisted from political events where he was speaking. His secretary sent an addendum to the $850 bill for my stay at

Mar-a-Lago, claiming they had forgotten to include the cost of the flight: $10,000. I even received a cryptic note late one night from a Republican opposition researcher, who told me someone had tried to hire him to investigate my personal life.

As Trump worked to undermine my reporting, he activated a network of right-wing noisemakers to assist in the cause. A Buffalo-based PR man named Michael Caputo circulated e-mails to Republican press secretaries warning that I was a "partisan flibbertigibbet" who could not be trusted. The *American Conservative*'s Jeffrey Lord wrote a comically long, line-by-line takedown of my story. Breitbart News churned out wall-to-wall coverage of the fracas, complete with a 2,100-word alternate-reality version of my trip to Mar-a-Lago: "EXCLUSIVE—TRUMP: 'SCUMBAG' BUZZFEED BLOGGER OGLED WOMEN WHILE HE ATE BISON AT MY RESORT." (In one particularly memorable passage, a Mar-a-Lago hostess identified as "Bianka Pop" recounted my attempts to seduce her: "He was looking at me like I was yummy . . . [like he wanted] a cup of me or something.")

The sheer volume of the smear campaign was impressive. At one point, scrolling down Breitbart's homepage yielded *seven* different stories related to my betrayal of "Mr. Trump"—photo after identical photo of my grinning face plastered across the website like "WANTED" posters in the Wild West.

For the most part, I found the episode amusing. No one in my personal life believed the lies, and no real professional damage was done. If anything, the temper tantrum I'd inadvertently provoked was helpful to my career. (When I had a book come out the next year, my publisher included some of Trump's tweets in the marketing material.)

Still, I found myself baffled by the strategy Trump and his allies had chosen to deploy. The lines of attack often seemed to contradict each other. In some stories, I was a nervous geek cowering in Trump's presence; in others, I was an aggressive boor harassing female hostesses. One day, Trump would dismiss me as an irrelevant "blogger" to be ignored, the next he would continue his Twitter barrage. What was the point of all this noise? Was anyone actually buying this?

In the years since my accidental vacation with Donald Trump, I've retold this story in countless venues, often using it to illuminate some aspect of his presidency—from his obsession with conspiracy theories to his outer-borough status anxiety.

Looking back now, though, what strikes me most about the experience was how closely it foreshadowed the way Trump would deal with the press from the Oval Office. His penchant for insulting disfavored reporters on Twitter is well-documented, of course. But the strategy is more sophisticated than that.

As president, Trump erected an elaborate messaging apparatus designed to undermine fact-based journalism and flood the American information ecosystem with propaganda. Every single day, on every platform, Trump and his allies waged war against "the enemies of the people." He led his supporters in ritualistic booing of the reporters at his rallies. He amplified attempts to discredit the press by outlets like Fox News and Breitbart. As I've reported for *The Atlantic,* pro-Trump political operatives scraped the social-media accounts belonging to hundreds of journalists and compiled the material into a dossier to be weaponized against any reporter who produces critical coverage. The Trump campaign filed libel lawsuits against the *New York Times,* CNN, and the *Washington Post.*

Many of the gadflies who Trump sent after me back in 2014 rose to power and prominence during his presidency. Caputo joined his campaign. Lord became a high-profile cable-news pundit. Steve Bannon, who ran Breitbart at the time, went on to become chief White House strategist. When Trump was a reality-TV personality, his crusade against me seemed goofy and ham-fisted. As commander-in-chief, waging a similar crusade against the entire institution of the press, the tactics felt slightly more ominous.

The goal wasn't to make people believe a certain set of facts. It was to exhaust and disorient them, to muddy the waters just enough that objective reality felt out of reach—whether it related to a phone call with the president of Ukraine, or the spread of a global pandemic, or a trip to Mar-a-Lago with a young reporter from BuzzFeed. "The Democrats don't matter," Bannon once said. "The real opposition is the media. And the way to deal with them is to flood the zone with shit."

McKAY COPPINS is a reporter for *The Atlantic*. He previously was a reporter for BuzzFeed News, for which he covered two presidential campaigns. He is the author of *The Wilderness: Deep Inside the Republican Party's Combative, Contentious, Chaotic Quest to Take Back the White House.*

THE STRAIGHT-TALKING LIAR

MARK LEIBOVICH

TO QUOTE MY FORMER executive editor, who put this book together, my assignment here is: to deliver fifteen hundred words on "how different (or not) reporting on President Trump and his administration is from reporting on other presidents and their administrations." I'll dispense with the cliff-hanger: It is indeed different. It is different in the same way that a horse sprouting wings and flying out the window would be different. This was clear from the moment Trump descended his gilded escalator and hijacked our politics, social-media feeds, and Thanksgiving meals, with no end in sight.

For me, the odyssey began with a few strange e-mails in spring 2015. I never had met Donald Trump, and doing so never held any particular appeal or urgency.

Naturally, I knew who he was, as Trump had always represented a certain fixture of our national furniture, for better or worse. But I never paid him any particular mind, never watched *The Apprentice,* never followed his divorces, feuds, or bankruptcies. Certainly I did not take him seriously as a presidential candidate. Like most people who follow politics for a living, I figured his campaign would amount to a brief squall, like one of those wild little blizzards that pop up out of nowhere in Iowa and then disappear just as suddenly. I resisted writing about Trump for as long as possible.

Then the e-mails started. The first one landed that summer, sent from "the Office of Donald J. Trump." A day earlier, I had been quoted in a throwaway *Politico* story about how much media attention Trump's campaign had been receiving. My point was to state what seemed obvious: that after Trump entered the race in June many reporters had expected his campaign to quickly fade or self-implode. That had not happened.

After the *Politico* story posted, I received a note, scanned and sent by e-mail, handwritten by Trump himself: "Mark, I never disappoint. Best wishes, Donald Trump."

After putting it off for much of the summer, I finally had no choice but to confront this growing beast of a story. Trump was not going away. So I was finally compelled (or "assigned," to be more precise) to write about his escalating offensive into our news habitats. Resistance was futile after a certain point.

In late August, I placed a call to the not-yet-famous Hope Hicks, Trump's ever-present press deputy. I asked her if I could talk to the candidate. Before Hope could relay the message, I received another note from Trump: "Mark, Time for a cover. Magazine looking good. Best wishes, Donald."

This would be my first brush with why covering Donald Trump was, in fact, not like covering the rest. Never before had a candidate, much less a celebrity front-runner, approached me like this, urging me directly— not through any aide—to get to work writing a cover story about him.

So, yes, this was unusual. It also defied the pose of cultivated sheepishness that presidential aspirants were expected to demonstrate at all times. In this regard, Trump's manic self-promotion could be oddly refreshing. I liked that he dispensed with the faux humility pose that most politicians strive for. I appreciated how Trump's campaign orbit was largely free of handlers and was very much his own production, down to his tweets— which he typed or dictated himself.

I also appreciated that gaining access to Candidate Trump was nothing at all like the teeth-gnashing exercise that it can be to get any meaningful exposure to a candidate like, say, Hillary Clinton. This was a seductive departure for political reporters accustomed to being ignored, patronized, and offered sound bites to a point of lobotomy by typical politicians and the human straitjackets that surround them. As I reported my story, Trump allowed me to join him all over—at his Trump Tower office and residence, in his limo, on his private jet, at his Trump National Golf Club in Rancho Palos Verdes, California, backstage at several TV interviews, and at the private cast party after he hosted *Saturday Night Live*. By allowing me to observe him in his various elements, Trump was positively shameless—a generally unflattering descriptor in most cases but also quite useful for my news-gathering purposes. He said all kinds of stuff that pols didn't usually let themselves say. He was transparent in the sense that Trump made no attempt to cloak his love of fame. He refused to traffic in that tiresome politicians' trope that his campaign is "not about me, it's about you."

"The ease with which Trump exhibits, and inhabits, his self-regard is not only central to his 'brand' but also highlights a kind of honesty about him," I wrote. The story—which ran on the cover of the *New York Times Magazine*—was headlined, "Donald Trump Is Not Going Anywhere."

"Honesty," of course, is a complicated notion where Donald Trump is concerned. It's true that countless supporters of Trump will attribute their love of him to his ability to convey a sense that he was leveling with them. That he was voicing truths that they themselves might subscribe to but would be afraid to say in public, for fear of offending the guardians of political correctness that Trump was railing against.

Yet Donald Trump also lied all the time. This was exhaustingly documented by journalists. He lied casually, unfailingly, and without remorse. It created a situation in which a candidate who had achieved a reputation among his supporters for straight talk was in fact spewing nonstop falsehood. This dichotomy—the straight-talking liar—has followed Trump on his extremely unlikely rise to the White House.

It is more than four years later, though it often feels like forty. President Trump does not grant much in-person exposure to journalists anymore, unless we happen to work for Fox News and are willing to cheerlead for him unabashedly. But the basic duality endures from the campaign, as does the same disconnect between how journalists see the world and how Trump's supporters do.

Yes, reporting on Trump is definitely "different" from anything I've experienced. People ask me all the time what it's like to be a reporter in a city where Trump looms over everything. I say there certainly are benefits. You sense a level of excitement because the story is so big and because people are tuned in and deeply invested in what we're doing. I am fortunate to work for an outlet—the *New York Times*—that has gained significant readership and revenues during the Trump years and accordingly has committed itself to hiring more reporters and supporting new and ambitious journalism.

Covering Trump is like covering a massive earthquake. There is so much material to work with. Our work feels exciting and relevant to people's lives. Theoretically this story provides just the kind of rush that seduced many of us into this business to begin with.

But it's also, well, an earthquake. It is scary and feels dangerous, and the full extent of the carnage to the world as we knew it will not be understood for years. Grave damage has been done to institutions, to norms, and certainly to the way people view journalists and consume journalism.

We've heard all of this, but here are some day-to-day examples of how my world has changed. The Washington bureau of the *New York Times,* where I come to work every day, employs a team of full-time, armed security guards. We receive threats and abuse all the time, much of it over social media, but also at political rallies, from self-appointed media vigilantes and even from the Trump White House itself.

The president tweeted a lot—also "different," if not inescapable. There are obvious downsides to this, as even his allies will concede: Trump's tweets were exhausting, often irresponsible, and in many cases just flat wrong and ridiculous. They fell well beneath many people's expectations of how a president should act. Journalists who covered the Trump White House regularly saw their days or nights—or lives—upended the second another tweet drops.

My own view is that, for as puzzling or even toxic as they can be, these tweets are a form of barely filtered access to the president. It's not as if the tradition of a White House press secretary delivering a daily briefing of talking points really advanced the cause of transparency that much. I expressed my support for Trump tweeting during the one in-person encounter I have had with him since he entered the White House.

In early June 2017, I stopped by to see Hicks, who at the time was working as the White House communications director. After about fifteen minutes of chatting in an ornate West Wing conference room, she asked me if I wanted to "say hello." I wondered to whom.

"POTUS," she said.

It's usually not this easy to infringe on the president's schedule. Sure, I said. Hope walked me in.

Trump was sitting alone in a small dining room just off the Oval Office at a table covered with papers. He half-stood when I walked in, said hello, and shook my hand. He immediately mentioned that "you treated me very badly" during the campaign, and that the "failing *New York Times*" had been "so unfair" to him. But the president was perfectly pleasant about it.

It was 12:30 p.m., and Trump was watching a recording of *Fox and Friends* from about four hours earlier. This was one of those stretches when Trump was tweeting a lot, including attacks on the mayor of London following a terrorist incident in that city the previous weekend. The tweets were becoming a growing topic of concern among Republicans, many of whom were urging him to stop. I urged him to keep it up.

Trump assured me that he would keep tweeting. "It's my voice," he said of Twitter, reminding me of how many millions of Twitter followers he had. "They want to take away my voice." That was not happening, he promised. Donald Trump was not going anywhere.

MARK LEIBOVICH is chief national correspondent for the *New York Times Magazine*. He is the author of four books, including *Big Game: The NFL in Dangerous Times* and *This Town,* the story of the "media industrial complex that is Washington."

LEARNING AND UNLEARNING POLITICAL JOURNALISM IN THE TRUMP ERA

REBECCA BUCK

LESS THAN ONE MONTH before Donald Trump would launch a presidential campaign to redefine campaigns, I stood inside the skeleton of his yet-unfinished Washington hotel, watching particles float down through the bright atrium, waiting to take the measure of the man and his ambitions.

Among the unpainted walls and construction detritus, I had arrived unknowingly at a line of demarcation. Before, I had covered politics as it was, as we all knew it to be. But that era was about to come crashing down, and from the rubble would emerge—what, exactly?

Trump arrived with a cluster of aides orbiting him like moons, a layer of dust glittering on the surface of his black leather dress shoes. He was distracted by questions about the hotel—the flagship restaurant design, how the rooms were coming along—and every few minutes he'd stop to bark a question at one of the moon men, projecting authority and decisiveness, all part of the act.

Only when the stage had been set, the character established for the audience, did Trump address the question of running for president. "I will tell you," he said conspiratorially, "I've already in my own mind very much made my decision."

We all know how that turned out. But, as I snapped my notebook shut that day, another consequential question lingered—unanswered, perhaps unanswerable. How should we cover a candidate who doesn't just break the mold, but blows it up?

There was no roadmap to consult, no answer key for this pop quiz.

Like Trump, reporters were making it up as we went along. To some extent, we still are.

Telling the story of American politics always has been an imprecise, fluid undertaking, more art than science. Because politics itself is constantly changing and evolving to fit the country's mood, the journalism that chronicles it must do the same. It is an eminently human endeavor—a living, breathing, imperfect thing.

In modern politics, the most successful national politicians have understood and harnessed changes in the media, while those who have been slow to adapt often have paid a price. Richard Nixon's sweaty upper lip wouldn't have mattered before the proliferation of television—but, in his 1960 debate meeting with John F. Kennedy, the image was broadcast on millions of screens across the country, inescapable and indelible.

In the 1980s, the rise of the "sound bite" vexed candidates like Michael Dukakis. "If you couldn't say it in less than 10 seconds, it wasn't heard because it wasn't aired," he vented after his unsuccessful 1988 bid for president.

Another seismic shift was underway even before the 2016 presidential election, as social media and the Internet further decentralized an already fractured media landscape. As former CNN reporter Peter Hamby wrote in a prescient 2013 Harvard paper, "Did Twitter Kill the Boys on the Bus? Searching for a better way to cover a campaign": "More and more, the mainstream political press is being cut out of the election process, raising questions about the value of being a reporter on the bus, on the plane, or 'in the bubble' with a presidential candidate."

Once solemn gatekeepers, reporters were wielding less access and influence than ever before—with public trust in the press eroding, and campaigns beginning to take their messages straight to voters. Trump recognized the trend even better than many in the media and, like successful candidates before him, he seized the moment for his own maximum benefit.

As a former reality-TV star, Trump also understood more intuitively than most the enduring power of television and the levers to manipulate it. Each day, he would offer up a new plot twist, often via Twitter, and watch the feeding frenzy ensue. Meanwhile, he tested the medium's limits, uttering more half-truths and outright falsehoods on live television than could realistically be fact-checked in real time.

Accountability mattered even less because Trump had a willing partner in one powerful cable network, which amplified and endorsed his message even when he diverged from the facts. His campaign and supporters could inhabit an alternate universe, and they often did.

In October 2016, I traveled to Ambridge, Pennsylvania, a diminished former steel town, for Trump's first rally following the bombshell release of archived *Access Hollywood* tapes, which captured Trump bragging to host Billy Bush about grabbing women's genitals prior to an interview. "When you're a star, they let you do it," Trump had said.

Republican officials frantically were jumping ship, condemning the comments, and withdrawing their support from Trump. But, in this corner of the Rust Belt, Trump's supporters either shrugged off his remarks or distrusted the story entirely.

"I think it was taken out of context," one supporter, Martin Radzanowski, said.

"I don't care what they catch on tape," another Trump supporter, Rick Wittmer, told me. ". . . I don't care what the news media says. They're on the other side. I don't listen to them."

This was a stunning, deeply clarifying moment: For a segment of the American public, I realized, the long-held conventions of politics and elections no longer applied.

We had watched this dynamic play out in myriad small and large ways with Trump over the course of the election, as the sacred butter cows of American politics melted before our eyes. Hadn't we believed retail politics was essential to a successful campaign? When Trump visited the Iowa State Fair, he bypassed the fabled soapbox and instead offered joyrides on his helicopter. Weren't debates a necessary test for would-be candidates? Trump skipped one, and voters didn't seem to mind.

Week by week, Trump exposed the emptiness of political rites we had treated like biblical commandments. Endorsements, can't-miss campaign stops, *basic facts*—none of it mattered, it seemed, except to the political establishment and the Washington–New York press.

As a young-ish journalist, I did not suffer from sepia-tinged memories of campaigns as they once were, with whistle-stop tours and candidates "on the hustings." But, like many other political reporters, I was drawn to the job because I *liked* politics. We all imagined writing our version of *What It Takes*, the Richard Ben Cramer opus set in the 1988 presidential election, or riding along on a modern-day Straight Talk Express— really getting to know a candidate, spending time with him, learning what makes him tick, and in so doing imparting important insights into his character.

Trump exposed that for what it had become: a relic and a fantasy.

Not that there wasn't value in learning about Trump or being out on the trail with him. In fact, for a candidate who was subverting the press, Trump was remarkably accessible and relished engaging with the media, particularly those he recognized from his favorite medium, television.

During a March 2016 press conference in Palm Beach, Trump zeroed in on me among the crowd of reporters, cutting off his response to a question. It had been a nearly a year since our interview in his hotel, but he recognized me from my analysis on cable news, including CNN.

"Oh, thank you for the nice things you always say about me," Trump said midstream, pointing me out from the crowd of reporters. "You are so nice. Thank you."

I felt the necks of the entire room swivel and sunk into my seat, wracking my brain for anything "nice" I might have said about the candidate. I must have turned a bright shade of red, or perhaps color drained from my face entirely, because Trump noticed my discomfort.

"Now she's going to be bad, because she's embarrassed," he added, addressing the room again. "But I just want to thank you."

After the event, as I was gathering my things, I turned to see Trump standing in front of me, waiting to shake my hand.

But Trump's obsession with television also made him more sensitive to it. By the end of the year, Trump—now the president-elect—would call CNN president Jeff Zucker to protest my on-air analysis. "He completely trashed her for two minutes, says, 'OK, got it?' and then hung up," Zucker later recounted to the *New York Times Magazine*.

I was lucky: Trump routinely targeted other journalists publicly. That practice, like many of his other successful but cynical tactics, since has been adopted more widely—as by Senator Martha McSally, who responded to a question by one of my CNN colleagues, Manu Raju, by calling him "a liberal hack." Soon, her reelection campaign was raising money off of the encounter.

Trump's impact on political journalism has not been limited to his own party, either. In the 2020 Democratic primary, Senator Bernie Sanders and his allies vocally criticized the "corporate media" for perceived bias and attempted to work around the system, speaking directly to their supporters.

Journalists have adapted, and continue to do so—but for whom? Subscriber numbers and television news ratings skyrocketed in the Trump era, suggesting as healthy a public appetite for political news as ever. Trust in the media, however, continued to slide. We are trying to speak to the whole of America, but narrower and narrower slices are listening.

And, after being slow to recognize these profound changes in the political and media landscape, we still are playing catch-up—still struggling to answer those fundamental questions about how to do what we do, now.

How do we cover campaigns when not only our nation's politics, but the fundamental building blocks of society, are seismically shifting beneath our feet? And how can a fractured media even begin to chart a clear path forward through the wilderness?

More than five years later, though, one thing seems clear: Trump didn't blow up political journalism. He just lit the fuse.

REBECCA BUCK is a CNN political reporter. She previously was a political analyst for CNN and a reporter for RealClearPolitics and the *Washington Examiner*.

WE ARE HIS OXYGEN— AND TORMENTOR

ASHLEY PARKER

THEY SAY YOU ALWAYS remember your first.

And so: The first time Donald J. Trump singled me out, by name, for heckling and derision, was at a massive rally in San Diego, more than five months before he was elected the forty-fifth president of the United States and just one day after he reached the number of delegates required to secure the Republican Party nomination.

Trump was about halfway through his speech when he suddenly turned his attention to a story by me and my then-colleague, Maggie Haberman, that had posted online several hours before he took the stage. (At the time, I was a political reporter for the *New York Times,* covering Trump; I joined the *Washington Post* to cover the Trump White House shortly after the 2016 election.)

"I just read a story by a woman named Parker and a woman named Haberman that's in the *New York Times,*" he said, before bemoaning that, rather than lauding his delegate victory the previous day, we had written about the stumbles and paranoia roiling his campaign as he struggled to transition from quixotic outsider to Republican Party standard-bearer.

I was sitting in the front row of the press pen, dead center of his 10,000-person rally, and I felt my cheeks flush pink. But Trump moved on, and I hoped the moment would pass.

It did not. About ten minutes later, he circled back to his anti–*New York Times* riff, training his focus anew on me and my co-byline.

"Who's with the *New York Times*?" Trump growled, pointing his right index finger as he swept his arm across the arena and squinted out into the dense crowd. "I hope it's not Maggie Haberman or Parker, because they are not legit. Where's the *New York Times* reporter? I call it the failing *New York Times*."

By now, the crowd was booing and hissing, twisting back toward the press pen to see if they could spot the "woman named Parker." A large, laminated sheet of paper bore my full name, which I discreetly tried to slip out of view and under my laptop, as I steadied my breathing and stared straight ahead—as if I, too, had no idea who these "not legit" reporters were.

That day in San Diego would not be the last time President Trump would single me out for criticism and attention. In my year covering him as a candidate for the *New York Times,* and my three-plus years covering him as a president for the *Washington Post,* Trump has mentioned me from the stage at a rally, tweeted about me and a colleague when he didn't like our story (dismissing us as "two nasty lightweight reporters" and threatening our White House credentials), and both needled and wooed me privately, from the Oval Office to Air Force One.

But it was the first time, and it did offer an early—and prophetic— glimpse of just how different Trump's relationship with the media would be, setting him apart from nearly every other president in modern history.

I hardly was the only one. Trump is particularly obsessed with some of the scribes from his hometown paper (the *New York Times*), as well as those he watches all day long on the large flat-screen TVs in the White House; MSNBC's Katy Tur—who Trump repeatedly dismissed as "Little Katy" when she was assigned to follow him around the country in 2016—chronicles what the spotlight was like in her book, *Unbelievable: My Front-Row Seat to the Craziest Campaign in American History.*

Trump can be particularly biting with female reporters, as well as reporters of color, but he has been harsh with men, too. During the campaign, cable networks hired personal protection for their on-air correspondents. Some who covered his campaign actively took themselves off the White House beat, not wanting to spend four—or possibly eight— more years in what they felt was a toxic brew. There were whispers of PTSD.

In short, the relationship between the president and his press corps is love-hate, with the president doing both the loving and the hating. He largely dictates the terms but also lives in our thrall, obsessing over our headlines, our stories, and what we say on cable news.

After the White House grandly proclaimed that it had cancelled its subscriptions to the *Washington Post* and the *New York Times*—and urged all federal agencies to do the same—Trump proudly held up a copy of the *Post* the day after the impeachment vote, brandishing the thick, black two-word headline: "Trump Acquitted." (In a meta-twist, a photo of Trump displaying that copy of the *Post* appeared the next day in . . . the *Post*.)

He desperately craves the approval of the media and has elevated the relationship to the emotional status of professional frenemyship.

In moments, he can be disarmingly accessible and charming. His tweets are real-time windows into exactly what he is thinking, at any moment, and, early in his presidency, it was not uncommon for reporters to be whisked suddenly into the Oval Office, simply because the president wanted to say hello and chat. (It is hard to overstate just how unheard-of this is; in any other administration, interviews and even informal conversations with the president often were negotiated in excruciating back-and-forths, weeks in advance.)

Trump is also the consummate host—the impresario of several private clubs, including Mar-a-Lago in Palm Beach, Florida—constantly trying to win over whoever is in front of him at any moment. When he occasionally appears in the press cabin of Air Force One, to chat with the traveling media, it is not uncommon for him to ask, "How are you doing? Are they taking care of you? Does anyone need anything to drink?"

And you almost feel that, in that moment, if you told the president that you were, in fact, a little thirsty, he himself would duck into the kitchen of the Boeing 747 and return bearing an icy Coke.

He even has led his traveling press corps to the front of his own cabin on Air Force One, to chat off the record—and, once, to watch a Democratic debate with him—brushing off the pleas of the airplane staff that we return to our seats for landing.

But he also has dubbed us the "FAKE NEWS" and "enemy of the people"—dangerous rhetoric being adopted by dictators and totalitarian rulers around the world—and made heckling the media and shouting "CNN sucks!" a staple of his campaign rallies.

We in the press are both Trump's oxygen and tormentor, and that has created a dynamic unlike any other.

At the *Post*, our former executive editor, Marty Baron, stressed that we don't cover Trump any differently than we'd cover any other president. But Trump did present different challenges.

Especially in the first year of his administration, when warring factions in the White House were trying to knife each other—often in the media—it could feel overwhelming to try to report out the objective truth. There were people with competing agendas, battling coalitions—remember the Nationalists versus the Globalists?—some earnest public servants and some proven liars, all trying to spin their narrative in the press in a roundabout attempt to influence the president.

I almost subconsciously grouped sources into categories. Some people never had lied to or misled me—at least that I was aware of—and this was the group I weighted most heavily. If they warned me that I had something wrong, or was missing a nuance, I went back and re-reported.

Other sources I viewed as Wikipedia-esque—a good jumping-off point, but nothing I ever would cite in, say, a term paper. In reporting terms, these were people who often had solid and intriguing tips, but ones I only would report if I could verify them with several other sources. And other people, still, I viewed as Reddit—prone to dizzying rabbit holes and misinformation but still occasionally useful.

Washington Post stories about this administration often included an all-but-trademarked line that goes something like this: "This portrait of the president in this moment is the result of interviews with twenty-seven administration officials, Republican lawmakers, aides, and confidants."

It's a bit of a mouthful, but the sentence served two important purposes—it offered some transparency to our readers, explaining to them that the story isn't based on one disgruntled aide with a vendetta, and it underscored the depth and breadth of our reporting. Especially in this era, we always endeavor to offer a kaleidoscopic view of the truth, as best we understand it.

Then there was the chaos of the Trump administration itself. We quickly learned that nearly every rumor and whisper needed to be run down, because sometimes the seemingly outlandish turned out to be true.

That Trump had referred to several African nations as "shithole countries" during a closed-door meeting? That Trump repeatedly had floated the idea of the United States trying to buy Greenland? That Trump privately—and then later publicly—talked about having the legal authority to pardon himself? True, true, true.

There also was the pace of his tweets, which could—and often did—come at all hours, especially in the wee dregs of the morning. The *Post,* for instance, has an extraordinarily large White House team—seven full-time reporters—as well as a virtually round-the-clock breaking-news team, which helped us handle the near-constant barrage of news emanating from the president.

Trump, meanwhile, christened the media "the Opposition Party." He said as much in tweets and speeches, and he tried to create a culture where an alien—trying to make sense of Earth for the first time—could be forgiven for thinking there are three political parties: Republicans, Democrats and the Opposition Media Party.

The effect was corrosive, and also at times confounding. Yes, I have been jeered and booed and dismissed. But depending on the audience—a book festival on Martha's Vineyard, say, or a panel in Seattle—I also have been praised and exalted.

People who recognize me from the *Washington Post* or from my appearances on TV—where I generally talk about my reporting at the *Post*—have come up to thank me and my colleagues for the work we're doing, and for holding the president accountable.

And while I appreciate the kind words—and am overjoyed to learn that people other than my family are reading my stories—I sometimes fear this represents a misunderstanding of the facts.

Yes, we do hold the president accountable—but that is because, as White House reporters, we hold *all* presidents accountable. Claim as Trump might, we are not the opposition party, to him or to anyone else.

As Marty Baron often said, "We're at work, not at war," and it's true: We are doing the hard work every day of covering every administration as rigorously, as thoroughly, and as fairly as we can.

That meant training our focus on President Trump. And we will continue to do that with any president. The specific dynamic may shift, but our mission will not.

So, for the current president or the President of Whom We Have Even Yet to Conceive: You may change, but our work continues.

ASHLEY PARKER is the White House bureau chief for the *Washington Post.* She formerly worked for the *New York Times,* covering the 2012 and 2016 presidential campaigns and Congress, among other assignments. She was part of the *Post* team that won the 2018 Pulitzer Prize for national reporting.

THE PRESS'S TRUMP CONUNDRUM

JILL COLVIN

"ARE THEY TAKING CARE OF YOU?" he asks.

"Are you comfortable?" he wants to know. "Can I get you anything? A Diet Coke?"

That's the Donald Trump you're likely to meet as a reporter sitting down with the president one-on-one. The longtime host and hotelier comes off as kind and complimentary, as if he just seated you at his finest table. He's self-effacing, funny. Undeniably charming.

It was one of the most stunning conundrums of the Trump presidency. He is a man who dangerously has villainized the press as "the enemy of the American people," using language that has been mimicked by dictators and incited violence against journalists in the United States and abroad.

It was a strategy that allowed him and his supporters to dismiss any reporting he deemed unflattering as "fake news." And it exacerbated a crisis of truth in this country, normalizing a wholesale assault on one of the few institutions left to check his power.

And, yet, no American president in modern history cared more about the press, consumed more news, spent more time interacting with reporters, or understood more acutely that the success of his administration depended to a large part on us.

He watched hours of cable news, using a fancy TiVo system to cue up dramatic exchanges, and reacted gleefully when one of his tweets jumps from his phone to the screen as "BREAKING NEWS." He read stacks of newspapers and printouts from online news outlets, studying his coverage and passing on critiques directly to writers in the form of Sharpie-scrawled notes or in-person commentary.

And he sized up his press corps, picking favorites and useful antagonists, while showing genuine respect for some, like veteran *New York Times* photographer Doug Mills, whom he praised to world leaders across the globe.

In the early days of the Trump administration, reporters had feared that the president would boot the press from its rundown but symbolic working space inside the White House West Wing, which gives reporters direct access to the offices of top administration press officials (along with the less-than-occasional mouse).

It turned out he liked us close. Especially in those first few weeks, reporters were on constant guard for Trump to summon us at a moment's notice when he had something he wanted to announce or a photo-op he wanted cameras to capture.

Since then, Trump continued his near-daily interactions with the press in the form of Oval Office "sprays," "gaggles" over the blaring rotor blades of Marine One as he departed the White House, and frequent off-the-record conversations with the small group of rotating reporters who travel with him aboard Air Force One. Those visits to the press cabin often happen suddenly, with no heads-up given to reporters. (I refused to use the bathroom on board for many months, terrified he'd suddenly materialize while I was locked inside.)

Often, it felt as if he just wanted to chat or gauge how news is playing. Once he invited the "fake news" up to his private cabin to watch the confirmation of his new Supreme Court justice; on another day, he led reporters, who do not have access to Wi-Fi on board, up front to watch highlights of a pivotal Democratic debate.

And Trump mastered the art of using the press, approaching his presidency like the director of a television drama, and ginning up a stream of constant controversy to keep himself on the front page.

We also were useful props. As he was competing in the Republican primaries, Trump took to holding his election-night victory parties at his various private clubs, inviting dues-paying members to witness the spectacle of his reaction speeches. Reporters would gather in ornately decorated ballrooms, complete with cherubs overhead, behind rows of club members, many of their faces tautly pulled and dripping with jewels for the occasion. It was a fun perk that helped justify rising membership rates; plus, it was easier for Trump to ignore questions from reporters seated twenty rows back.

Later, Trump invited the traveling press to cover the ticketed New Year's Eve party he hosts each year at Mar-a-Lago, where aging celebrities such as Sylvester Stallone and romance-novel cover model Fabio mingle with Palm Beach's social set.

In a tradition that continued through his presidency, club staff set up a red carpet near the ballroom's entrance and positioned the press alongside it, offering his guests a paparazzi experience, complete with news photographers flashing and reporters shouting questions as guests mug for the cameras.

And it's a two-way street. Even as he undermined the press, launching unprecedented attacks on individual reporters and news outlets, Trump was good for the news business when it comes to viewers and clicks.

A former reality-TV-show host, Trump knows how to put on a show. There's endless palace intrigue, hypocrisy, scandal. And, while other presidents have sought to keep their private thoughts private, Trump's Twitter feed provided an open window to an id reeling with grievances, engaged in endless self-soothing as he longs for approval. He'd take nearly any question shouted his way, even as he killed the White House press briefing for a time, turning reporters who once raised their hands to be called on into rabid animals shouting over helicopter rotor blades.

And he elevated the reporters who cover him, inspiring Pulitzer Prize–winning coverage and turning once-disheveled print reporters into cable-news pundits, with some earning lucrative cable-news contracts and major book deals—along with tweeted attacks, endless (and often disturbing) hate mail, and sometimes death threats.

When Trump, in November 2015, tweeted that I was "one of the truly bad reporters" and that my stories were "fictional garbage," I knew it was a badge of honor. And, yet, the tweet—still in the early days of his campaign when his attacks on reporters were less common and more transparent—filled me with dread. What was he mad at? Had I done something wrong? And couldn't he at least have gotten my Twitter handle right so I could have earned a flood of new followers? Now, the tweet sits in my apartment, framed.

JILL COLVIN covers the White House for the Associated Press. She began her journalism career at the *New York Daily News,* where one of her first assignments was to stake out a property owned by Donald Trump in Westchester County, New York, where workers were constructing an elaborate Bedouin tent—complete with a goat—for former Libyan dictator Muammar Gaddafi in case he needed a place to stay during the UN General Assembly. The town was not happy.

II

COULD ALL OF THIS BE OUR FAULT?

FROM FOUR PROMINENT JOURNALISTS, the answer is yes. Frank Sesno, formerly of CNN and now at George Washington University, writes a prescription for cable news to improve. Carl Cannon of RealClearPolitics and Charlie Cook of the *Cook Political Report* worry that bias seeps into so much of what journalists do. Tom Rosenstiel of the American Press Institute fears that journalists will "take the bait" of President Trump and become an opposition force. All have sobering reflections—which many journalists will not want to hear.

COVER THE CONSEQUENCES

It's Time to Retool the White House Beat

FRANK SESNO

IN MY BASEMENT, in a big plastic storage crate marked "Photos and memorabilia," I dig through pictures and press passes, old scripts and reporter notebooks. I find a legal-size folder, browning just a bit around the edges. "Statements/briefings" the label reads. Inside: the transcript I'm looking for. Slightly brittle now, with my fading margin notes and yellow highlights still marking what I considered the most newsworthy quotes, the transcript preserves a moment the way only a hard-copy document can. It was there, an eyewitness to events, a tangible connection, now preserved on this analog relic from another time.

The White House
Office of the Press Secretary
For Immediate Release November 25, 1986

The president had come to the briefing room to make a stunning announcement to the hastily assembled and slightly breathless press corps. The transcript records the time as 12:05 p.m. EST. "Last Friday, after becoming concerned whether my national security apparatus had provided me with a . . . complete factual record with respect to the implementation of my policy toward Iran, I directed the Attorney General to undertake a review of this matter over the weekend and report to me on Monday."

I remember the moment vividly. I was sitting in the fourth row, second seat in from the aisle, in that famously cramped briefing room. I was a too-young White House reporter, in over my head, but deliriously challenged by covering this most consequential place at a time of high drama and epic confrontation in the world—Cold War, nuclear rearmament, surrogate wars, and diplomatic dances around the globe. From the Middle East to the Caribbean, from Africa to Asia, the United States was flexing its considerable muscle. Now something had gone terribly wrong. And the world was watching.

CNN was coming into its own. The audience was growing, not yet sliced and diced into digital narrowcasts and microtargeted demographics. My job was to report and inform. Most reporters I knew felt the same way. They conveyed information and facts—and felt a responsibility to hold those they covered accountable for their words and actions. The president of the United States tacitly acknowledged all of that when he stepped in front of the microphone that day. I kept the notes to prove it.

The words were stunning and unexpected. They raised the curtain on a scandal that nearly derailed Ronald Reagan's presidency. An arms-for-hostages scheme run by top officials at the National Security Council, who then funneled "profits" to anti-communist rebels in Nicaragua. Iran-Contra was a flagrant violation of the law and a political disaster. Investigative reporting and congressional hearings revealed damaging details. The president's job approval plummeted. Ultimately, reluctantly, he would tell the nation "mistakes were made."

But, on that day in November, the president called out the problem and said it raised "serious questions of propriety." No one knew where it would all go. "Determination of the full details of this action will require further review and investigation by the Department of Justice," he said.

There it was. From the top. A call for an investigation. Conducted by the Justice Department. Intended to ferret out the facts and the wrongdoers. On the spot, the president announced that the national security adviser and his deputy, Lieutenant Colonel Oliver North, who had run the operation, were out. Accountability. "I'm going to ask Attorney General Meese to brief you," the president concluded, recognizing that the public had a right to know and the news media had a job to do.

For the next year, there was spin, denial, and political posturing. Some news stories hyped the facts, some got parts of the story wrong. But no one called the investigation a hoax, and no one suggested that the coverage, which headlined plenty of bad and embarrassing news, was fake.

That was then. Donald Trump's approach to the media, to those who cover him, to facts and oversight and investigation, flipped on its head the notion of accountability, transparency, and a healthy, if strained, relationship with the press. Trump branded reporters who dared challenge him "dishonest." Bad news was a "hoax." Investigations were "witch hunts." He used social media to go over the heads of mainstream media to his loyal base and shape his narrative through constant attack and sheer volume. He has served as his own spokesman and showed that the daily press briefing, where press secretaries actually can provide detail and context, is optional. Where other presidents have viewed the press as a troublesome but fundamentally healthy check on power, Trump got mileage out of undermining the very premise of its work.

Future presidents almost certainly will ratchet down the rhetoric. But they will study Trump's playbook. They will see that they can drive the news cycle through assertive use of social media, rally their base with every tweet, and use the White House as not merely the bully pulpit but as a reality show that pushes one news cycle into the next with dizzying and intentionally distracting ferocity.

How then can the media, especially always-on cable news, keep up with the relentless and changing demands of the beat, hold the president accountable, and not get drawn into news traps that have become so easy to set? How can digital media rise to the challenge and assume a greater place at the information table? How should traditional news organizations capitalize on the appetite and need for a healthier White House news diet?

I offer a road map, imperfect and incomplete, but intended to guide an approach to presidential coverage that is responsive both to the media-political landscape and to the public that journalism should serve. I offer this list knowing that ratings, clicks, and eyeballs matter, and that unless someone comes up with a different business model, news organizations must make money. I concede that talk shows, panels, and commentary often are compelling and successful. But I believe that we can feed the beast while also nourishing the brain. We can marry solid journalism with compelling storytelling. We can take creative advantage of social-media platforms and evolving technologies.

There are several waypoints on this road map. Start with a simple, overarching premise: First, cover the consequences. This would represent a substantial shift from the who's up, who's down palace intrigue, the Twitter-gazing that came to dominate so much of the coverage during the Trump presidency. Of course, we still need aggressive reporting to track the hard-news developments of the day and the assault on political norms. But sustained coverage of the consequences of presidential decisions would substantially broaden White House reporting. The consequences of a border wall, of trillion-dollar deficits, of record-low unemployment, of a military strike that killed an Iranian general who had targeted Americans and others. Covering the consequences means following up, sticking with the story. Consequences can be positive, negative, or occupy gray space in between. Next, dive into the regulatory realm. For decades, presidents have been increasingly asserting themselves, bulking up executive power. President Obama imposed hundreds of new executive orders and regulations. The Trump administration launched an ambitious campaign to roll them back. The Brookings Institution's Deregulation Tracker reveals the reach that the White House can have. Just a few of the regulations the Trump administration sought to challenge or change: designating undocumented immigrants for expedited removal, homeless transgender protections, the Coal Ash Rule, hunting and sportfishing regulations, the Clean Air Act, implementation of the Fair Housing Act, the Clean Power Plan, the Endangered Species Act, state requirements for Medicaid beneficiary access, fire extinguishers for recreational vessels, state funding for abortion providers, net neutrality, firearms prohibition for the mentally disabled.

Reporters should use this list as a primary source for their coverage: It offers a trove of potential story ideas that would inform news consumers about what the president and his administration are doing. What actually happens when Internet privacy rules are loosened? Who are the winners and the losers? What about firearms for the mentally disabled? Child nutrition? Migratory birds? Calorie labeling? The Clean Air Act? Coal ash? Each of these calls out for reporting and follow-up. Each invites stories about people—mothers, fathers, children, workers, asylum seekers, entrepreneurs, investors, sick, poor, middle class. Who are they, what are their stories, how are these moves by the government affecting them?

Covering the consequences can help prioritize editorial decision-making. Done right and across political parties, it can shed light on vitally important stories and deliver ratings and clicks.

Some other points on the map:

Organize the consequence coverage around three Ps: proposals, promises, and policy. They can be followed over time, turned into strong stories about commitments fulfilled and broken, services delivered and denied. Even in a world of emotion and outrage, results matter and provide an editorial approach that can engage reporters, sources, and the public alike.

Do the data. With an astonishing amount of data easily obtainable, stories can be told clearly and visually. Building effective digital narratives around data provides rich opportunities to do enterprise reporting that news consumers will see as driven by quantifiable fact. Flu deaths, car safety, taxes, crime rates among immigrant versus native-born populations, the uses of foreign aid, income inequality—all of these can be illustrated and brought to life through data-driven storytelling.

Double down on fact and reality checks. Yes, continue to call out the flips, flops, disinformation, lies, and the rest of the malicious stuff in the information junkyard. It stinks! These fact and reality checks will be more important as deep fakes and other deceptive digital practices become more prevalent. There even could be a fact-check game show or app. Watch the commentary, expand the cast of characters. On television, radio, and across the digital landscape, commentary and talk are easily produced and are proven audience draws. But it's often the same people, saying the same things. Broaden the conversation by bringing in different people from different places with different real-life experiences. From Kansas and Oregon, Alabama and Michigan, New Hampshire and New Mexico. Serious news organizations can elevate their analysis and commentary by using set-up pieces or interstitial elements to convey factual, baseline information, context, or relevant history.

Get out of the White House. Often, the best way to cover the White House is to leave it. Departments, agencies, interest groups, states, cities, towns are filled with people who want to talk and stories waiting to be told. Social media is a powerful force. Getting out of the White House, whether physically or virtually, to listen to people with a diverse range of experience enriches any reporter and brings perspective to a beat that often feels hermetically sealed.

And finally: Where there is agreement, recognize it, cover it. Don't minimize the controversies, scandals, and lies, but the focus of White House coverage should not be all-war-all-the-time. Don't be the buzzard at the barbeque circling only for the trash and the scraps.

Donald Trump changed the rules of White House coverage. His personal attacks on reporters, his dismissal of anything that runs counter to his version of events, his assault on facts and decency have made what once was the most prestigious beat in journalism the most contentious. Yet covering the place is more important than ever, a vital and daily check on presidential power. It is a mission that goes well beyond Donald Trump and will extend past his presidency.

The new model of White House coverage needs to be more substantive and more adept, imaginative, and focused on actions, not words. Reporters need to wake up every morning promising themselves not to go down rabbit holes of distraction.

It's time to reimagine and refocus the journalism that tracks the most powerful person in the world. And cover the consequences.

FRANK SESNO covered the White House for AP Radio and CNN and was CNN's Washington bureau chief. He served as director of the School of Media and Public Affairs at George Washington University in Washington, DC, and now is the director of strategic initiatives there. He also is a professor at GW. He is the author of *Ask More: The Power of Questions to Open Doors, Uncover Solutions, and Spark Change.*

BRONX CHEERS FROM AND FOR THE PRESS BOX

CARL M. CANNON

DURING PRESIDENT TRUMP'S first year in office, I attended a press briefing at the Jefferson Hotel. Situated on Sixteenth Street in Washington, the hotel affords a classic view of the White House, and I left the event with two men who once worked there, Michael Gerson and Peter Wehner. Without any preamble, one of them asked me, "Are you worried?"

I understood the question. I also understand how hard it is for them to stomach President Trump. Both are evangelical Christians who take their faith seriously. Perhaps better-known today as columnists—Mike for the *Washington Post* and Pete for the *New York Times*—both worked for George W. Bush, whom they admire.

"Yeah, this guy is worrisome," I said. "But I'm *more* concerned about what you guys are doing. What we in the media are doing."

They seemed taken aback and asked me to explain. I told them that Donald Trump would leave office someday and take his New York insult-comic sensibilities with him, but I feared that journalism never would return to its old norms: That the openly hostile coverage he's generated—the *ad hominem* attacks, the open partisanship in newsrooms, the demonization of his aides, appointees, and even his voters—that none of this will end when Trump leaves.

"You should write that," Gerson said quietly. Pete, who is a friend, agreed even though he considered Donald Trump a menace. I replied that I gently had been making that case, in one form or another, for two years—without making a ripple. "Maybe you're being too subtle," one of them quipped in a self-deprecating allusion to his own decidedly unsubtle anti-Trump columns.

Criticizing the only industry I've known in my professional life—the one I was raised in—isn't easy. But when Jerry Ceppos called and explained this project, I decided to say my piece. To be blunt, I believe that, collectively, we're as bad as Trump. I believe our behavior helped bring him to power in the first place.

I didn't initially feel this way. Posted in Washington since Ronald Reagan's presidency, I covered the White House for fifteen years and was only passingly familiar with the New York businessman, reality-television host, and tabloid fodder. I found Trump obnoxious but irrelevant to my life. That changed on June 16, 2015, when he made his presidential announcement from Trump Tower. I recoiled at this performance, especially when he blathered about Mexico sending its "rapists" to America. I was cohosting a SiriusXM radio program with RealClearPolitics founder Tom Bevan back then, and on the radio that day I called the speech "racist." Tom was startled. I'm careful when I discuss politics and have been nonpartisan my entire adult life, in private as well as in public.

But, as the 2016 GOP primary season heated up, Trump continued to voice many such shameful and specious assertions. Like my colleagues, I tried to set the record straight when possible. In mid-February, one of my Sunday columns was headlined, "Donald Trump, Iraq Demagogue." Here's how it began:

Perhaps you believe, as do a slight majority of the American people, that the 2003 US invasion of Iraq was a mistake. You may also believe, as I do not, that Donald Trump's willingness to avoid the clichés and rigidity that embody modern politics earns him a pass for slandering Mexicans, Muslims, women, journalists, the handicapped, and US Navy pilots shot down over Vietnam.

But Trump is now spewing nonsense about Iraq that demonstrates why the mere thought of him as commander-in-chief is so appalling. . . . In Saturday night's debate, the real estate tycoon invoked his singular rhetorical style to pronounce the US military involvement in Iraq "a big, fat mistake." He then added that George W. Bush and his top advisers deliberately took the country into war under false pretenses. "They lied," Trump said. "They said there were weapons of mass destruction—there were none. And they knew there were none."

If this were true, it would have been an impeachable offense, possibly an international war crime. In regurgitating conspiracy theories usually heard in the fever swamps of the far left, Trump reminds us that any globe is round—and that the baying hounds on the extreme right and extreme left often meet on the dark side of the moon.

My friends enjoyed this column. Pete Wehner tweeted that it was "a marvelous takedown by a terrific journalist." I appreciated the kind words, but it was a critical e-mail from someone I don't know that got my attention. Instead of the typical name-calling, this writer made a succinct point about news coverage critical of Trump.

"Of course, you don't like this," he wrote. "It's aimed at you."

I thought about that a great deal as the campaign unfolded. It suggested that the Trump phenomenon was a reaction to something. But what? In the best line of 2016 campaign coverage, Salena Zito would point out that Trump's supporters took him seriously, if not literally, while the media did the opposite. But that wasn't the last word on the subject. Millions of American voters not only ignored media criticism of Trump, they had concluded that we were part of the problem. As president, Trump shockingly would call us the "enemy of the people"—even as a Saudi journalist was murdered and dismembered in a consulate in a NATO country—but he was talking this way from the start of his campaign.

"They're scum," he called us in Atkinson, New Hampshire. He repeated that word three times in South Carolina, adding, "Totally dishonest people." In Grand Rapids, Michigan, he said this: "I would never kill them, but I do hate them."

All that was in 2015. This is not the way a decent—or even mentally healthy—public servant should talk. But, as the campaign unfolded, it raised a couple of questions: First, are any of his grievances valid? Second, why was there such a ready audience for these kinds of attacks on the media?

Let's take the second question first. While I don't have the space to document decades of media bias against conservatives, I will point to an example from 2008, a year when Trump wrote checks supporting Hillary Clinton's campaign. The setting was the vice-presidential debate between Sarah Palin and Joe Biden in St. Louis. Ignoring a lifetime of Biden malapropisms, the press had concluded that Palin was an airhead. In their debate, however, she held her own. Biden was the dunce. He erroneously asserted that John McCain voted with Barack Obama on a budget resolution and derided McCain for opposing a test-ban treaty "that every Republican has supported." (In fact, fifty-one out of fifty-five GOP senators voted against it.) Biden preemptively gave Pakistan intercontinental missiles, claimed the United States and France had "kicked Hezbollah out of Lebanon," and denied that Obama ever said he'd sit down with Iran's leaders. All that was wrong, and the last one was weird: In the primaries that year, Biden criticized Obama for his Iran gambit, calling him "naive."

Biden prefaced one howler by telling Palin, "With Afghanistan, facts matter"—before claiming that the United States was spending "more money in three weeks on combat in Iraq than we spent on the entirety of the last seven years that we have been in Afghanistan." His math was off by 2,000 percent. A former Senate Judiciary Committee chairman, Biden also mangled the constitutional history of the vice presidency. It reminded me of John Belushi in *Animal House*. ("Was it over when the Germans bombed Pearl Harbor? Hell, no!") I wrote that, too, but, as far as I know, I was the only one who panned Biden's fact-free debate performance.

Voters don't necessarily know the details of Article II of the US Constitution, or how far Pakistan can project its nuclear capabilities, but they do know when the press takes sides, as we did in 2008. Except for the most committed political partisans, they don't like it. By the time Donald Trump came along, we already had squandered our credibility. When Ronald Reagan ran for president, he was routinely derided as a racist, someone whose bellicose attitude toward the Soviet Union was likely to start World War III. *Los Angeles Times* cartoonist Paul Conrad depicted Reagan as a young Hitler, planning a fascist putsch in a darkened Munich beer hall.

We labeled George H. W. Bush, who volunteered for combat at age eighteen, a "wimp." We depicted George W. Bush, with degrees from Harvard and Yale, as a borderline illiterate, and the gentle Mitt Romney as a vulture capitalist who killed people. John McCain didn't just have a temper: we hinted that he was mentally unhinged from his time as a Vietnam

War POW. But if every Republican is a dummy—and you've compared the genial Reagan to Adolf Hitler—what's left in your arsenal that any open-minded person could credit?

The upshot: When Donald Trump comes along and we level all of the above criticisms at him while calling him an existential threat to democracy, a large swath of voters had long ago tuned us out. "Don't be surprised," warned Russ Schriefer, a Romney adviser, "when your accusations against Trump are falling upon deaf ears and aren't working, when you've used them in the past against a person for whom the descriptions didn't fit."

But, if we played a key role in getting Trump elected, we still had to cover him, which presented all kinds of other problems. He hated the press long before Inauguration Day—the feeling was mutual—and he presented us with an immediate stink bomb by instructing his White House press secretary to lie about the size of the inauguration crowds, of all things. It's been all downhill from there.

CNN, which apparently felt institutional guilt for giving the Donald unlimited free airtime during the campaign, went full bonkers by putting Stormy Daniel lawyer Michael Avenatti (now a convicted felon) on air an astonishing 121 times. He was on MSNBC 108 times. By 2019, I had feelings of déjà vu. I'd wake up and find that, in the middle of the night, Trump had done, said, or tweeted two or three controversial things. These ranged from sensible conservative policies to insane rants. They'd all be treated the same on *Morning Joe,* with the guests trying to outdo one another with—dare I say it?—Trumpian insults. CNN and the major newspapers, as if auditioning to be the house organ of "the Resistance," would join the fray. By midmorning, Trump's misbehavior would be exaggerated and mischaracterized to the point where you found yourself wondering what he'd actually done and whether it was really that bad.

It all starts again the next morning. It's worse than "Groundhog Day." Unlike Bill Murray's Phil Connors, I can't do anything to make the day bearable.

I certainly understand how Trump challenges our traditional journalistic forms. He casually lies about meaningless things, and important things. He's ignorant of American history. He alienates US allies while kissing up to dictators. He boasts like an emotionally maladjusted eight-year-old and belittles anyone around him. He's crude and mean. In the first three years of his presidency, we documented all this to no visible effect on his approval rating—until he flubbed the White House response to the coronavirus pandemic. So, what to do? One day early in his tenure, I was urging my writers to trust the process—to keep our heads even while everyone was losing theirs.

"I know what you mean," one of them said, "but you're asking me to legitimize him."

I replied that it was the Founders—and their Electoral College—who had "legitimized" Trump. What she meant was that treating Trump as we would a normal politician is what "normalizes" him. I get that, but what's the alternative? Back in the 1980s, when I was a regional correspondent in the old Knight Ridder newspapers' Washington bureau, I was asked at the last minute to help cover a San Francisco 49ers–Washington Redskins game. I arrived at the media section in RFK Stadium just as 'Niners quarterback Joe Montana scrambled for a first down. "Yes!" I shouted.

"No cheering in the press box," a chorus of voices sang out.

It was the first time I'd heard the phrase and, wishing to save face, I wisecracked, "I'm not cheering. I have money on the game," which made the old-timers smile. Still, I've never forgotten the lesson. But that's not how we cover the news today. There's plenty of cheering in the press box. Booing, too. And name-calling, heckling, and worse.

Is it justified when it comes to Trump? On the merits, yes, some of it is justified. But at what cost to ourselves and the country? "Whoever fights *monsters,*" Friedrich Nietzsche once cautioned, "should look to it that he himself does not become a *monster.*"

In 2017, Steven Spielberg produced a wonderful movie about the Pentagon Papers. He chose to set it in the *Washington Post* newsroom, rather than the *New York Times*'s, which actually broke the story. Meryl Streep was her typical brilliant self as Katharine Graham. Tom Hanks did a terrific Ben Bradlee. At one point, Bradlee wants to know what the *Times* is planning, so he dispatches a copy aide to New York City and tells him to sneak into the *Times* newsroom and keep his ears open.

"Is that legal?" says the wide-eyed young man.

"What is it you think we do here for a living, kid?" Bradlee growls. The unspoken answer is we find the news and we print it.

This ethos has not survived the Trump presidency. In 2019, the *Times* refused to publish the name of a "whistleblower" who ratted out Trump over his problematic phone call with the Ukraine president. I'm all about protecting news sources, but this guy wasn't the *Times*'s source. He was Adam Schiff's source. Not one newspaper in this country was willing to name the guy. Republicans came to believe it was because doing so would undermine the Democrats' narrative that he was a loyal public servant rather than a partisan plant inside the White House. I don't know which view is right. I do know that the whistleblowing statute was designed to protect government employees who ferret out graft to report it without losing their jobs. It doesn't contemplate being able to get a president impeached without ever having your name in the newspaper.

The Russia scandal revealed the problem of having a press as partisan and polarized as our two major political parties. There are two worldviews of what transpired. The first is that Donald Trump has an oddball antipathy for Ukraine, a Russia adversary, and an even wackier affinity for Vladimir Putin that he's never bothered to explain to the American people. And that Russia pulled all kinds of dirty tricks on social media—not to mention hacking Democratic Party e-mail accounts—in an effort to help Trump win. And that the Trump campaign welcomed this help and may have encouraged it.

Here's the competing narrative: That partisan officials in a thoroughly politicized FBI (and CIA) who had demonstrated a loathing for Trump and a desire to see Hillary Clinton elected interfered with the election by spying on his campaign, falsifying documents to get search warrants, and leaking material about Trump to the press that they knew was untrue—and lied about the whole enterprise for four years, first in an effort to prevent his election and, later, to try and remove him from office.

I'm not sure which view is closer to the truth. There are facts in support of both, and they are not mutually exclusive. But I do know that suspicion of FBI snooping on Americans once was a shared value by every liberal in this country. I shared it always, and still do. I haven't forgotten that for decades the bureau spied on so many Americans because of their politics, including members of my own family—and on an array of luminaries admired in our household: from Ernest Hemingway, Dorothy Parker, and Ring Lardner, to Cesar Chavez, Muhammad Ali, and Martin Luther King Jr. Marilyn Monroe, too. And Ben Bagdikian—over the Pentagon Papers.

I also know that, with few exceptions, today's media have been incurious on the question of overreach by the FBI and the nation's intelligence agencies. Not only have we failed to present both sides of this great argument, we have pretended as if there is only one legitimate side. We don't *even acknowledge the other side,* except when dismissing it as "lies" or the purview of Deep State "conspiracy" theorists. And that's how we've normalized Donald J. Trump: by acting just like him. By having no sense of our own history. By dismissing inconvenient story lines as "fake news." By calling the other side names and throwing tantrums when we lose an argument. We are him. He is us.

CARL M. CANNON is Washington bureau chief of RealClearPolitics and executive editor of Real Clear Media Group. He is the author or coauthor of seven books, including *On This Date: From the Pilgrims to Today, Discovering America One Day at a Time.*

THE DOWNFALL OF JOURNALISM

CHARLIE COOK

MORE THAN A FEW PEOPLE have said that they worry about what President Trump has done to our country. Whether I share that view is not relevant, but I do have concerns that news coverage of the Trump presidency has caused great damage to the profession of journalism and the credibility of the news media and threatens to do more.

This essay is an expression of concern that the reputation for impartiality of my profession of thirty-six years is in grave danger. Being seen as evenhanded is essential for the media to play its important role in our society. This is not a screed by a Republican or a conservative. I am neither, instead an independent and fairly moderate. This is not in any way a defense of Trump.

The credibility of the news media is predicated on a perception of absolute impartiality. My concern is that the self-inflicted damage to the profession and to the unique role that the media are supposed to provide will remain. The more people question the evenhandedness of the media, the more corrosion occurs on the underpinnings of the profession and the vital role that journalism is supposed to play in a free society. Once virginity is lost, it never is restored. Once the integrity of the media and of journalism is lost, it will be a long time before it can, if ever, be restored.

The Gallup Organization began measuring trust in the media in 1972, asking a sample of American adults, "In general, how much trust and confidence do you have in the mass media—such as newspapers, T.V. and radio—when it comes to reporting the news fully, accurately, and fairly—a great deal, a fair amount, not very much, or none at all?" In 1972, 68 percent said they had "a great deal "or "fair amount" of trust and confidence. The combined great deal/fair amount totaled 69 percent in 1974 and 72 percent in 1976.

In September 2019, the combined great deal/fair amount had dropped 27 points since 1972, to 41 percent. According to Gallup, fewer than one in seven Republicans and one in four self-described conservatives in 2019 reported having a great deal or a fair amount of trust and confidence.

But this loss of confidence is not confined to Republicans and conservatives. Barely more than one in three independents and fewer than half of moderates reported having a great deal or fair amount of trust in the media. These are hardly groups that are staunchly pro-Trump. They are relatively nonaligned but have lost much of whatever trust they had in the media.

On the other hand, almost seven in ten Democrats and a bit fewer than two out of three liberals had a great deal or fair amount of confidence in the media. When one party or faction is delighted with the media, that is a time for the media to worry.

It is the intensity of the animosity or lack of trust that should be most disconcerting. Almost half of Republicans and more than four in ten conservatives reported having no confidence in the media. A little less than a third of independents and almost one in four moderates had no confidence. Conversely, only one in ten Democrats and one in seven liberals had no confidence.

The September 2019 Gallup report said, "Republicans became increasingly mistrustful of the media in 2016 when Trump was campaigning for president and was sharply critical of the media's coverage of him. Between 2015 and 2016, *Republican trust in the mass media fell 18 points* to its historic low of 14 percent, where it remained in 2017. Following a seven-point boost last year, it has returned to 15 percent. For their part, Democrats consistently have been more trusting of the media than Republicans but rallied around the press and *became even more trusting when Trump took office in 2017.*"

The profession and news organizations have a problem, but it is not obvious how well that is understood among those in the business. Journalists are good at carefully listening to public figures. But many of these same journalists seem oblivious to how their own words are perceived by others. To many in the media, the idea that anyone would question their fairness and evenhandedness is unimaginable.

They see themselves as scrupulously impartial and cannot begin to understand how anyone could feel otherwise. It is not just conservatives and Republicans who long have had a distrust of the media. It also exists among independents, who naturally have a mistrust of institutions. The danger is that news organizations and journalists are being seen not as impartial observers but as participants, combatants in the political battles, with little question in the minds of many about which color uniform they are wearing on the battlefield.

Obviously, the worlds of politics and the media are far more complicated and challenging than they used to be. The Pew Research Center in January 2020 released a study, "U.S. Media Polarization and the 2020 Election: A Nation Divided," documenting where Americans are seeking their political news and, in many cases, self-perpetuating and reinforcing the walls of their ideological and partisan silos, a trend that objective journalists should worry about.

We hear relatively new terms like "negative partisanship" and "political tribalism." The first describes the animosity that more and more voters have toward the other party and its leaders. Many partisans believe that there is little if anything that the other party would not stoop to, hence the anticipation for those out of power of an "October Surprise," a deliberate and improper action by the governing party to influence the outcome of an upcoming election. At the same time, these partisans are willing to afford their own party and its leaders every benefit of the doubt.

The second term describes the rise of the binary view that every issue or subject is "us vs. them." Someone is either on your team or in the opposition; there is no room for anything in between. These concepts are being extended to how journalism is perceived, that any article that is not critical of the other party or is critical of a member of your tribe, is by definition biased. This is the environment of mistrust in which journalists must operate.

A Knight Foundation/Gallup study in 2018 confirmed how challenging many people believe it is to pick through what is true and untrue.

Looking at the research on trust, a journalist might understandably ask, "What are we doing that so thoroughly alienates such a large proportion of Americans and leaves a disturbing number of others with an unhealthy degree of skepticism?" Or, "Where will they seek news and information if they don't trust us?" My impression is that few, or not enough, in the media understand those questions.

In my Captain Shreve High School journalism class fifty years ago, we were taught the four Ws, "who," "what," "when," and "where." We were told to stay away from "why," to not explicitly attempt to judge the veracity of statements or assign motives to actions. But we also were told to make it apparent when a reader, listener, or viewer might want to take note. I don't recall where "how" came into play, but care should be taken in that as well. We were taught to stick to the basics, report the facts, and let readers draw their own conclusions. I recall Mrs. Lawson telling our class that "editorializing belongs on the editorial page." We were told that opinions and judgments did not belong in a news story. Period. Call me old-fashioned, but to me what we were taught in that Shreveport, Louisiana, classroom is more important now than ever.

With all of this in mind, I was disturbed to read news reporting from several of the most important and respected news organizations in the world employing terms such as "this is untrue" or "this is false" or "a lie," in reference to statements by President Trump and his administration. These are journalistic cardinal sins, regardless of whether the characterization is true. The only times such terms should be used in a news story is in quoting someone else.

No serious person is suggesting that reporters unquestioningly regurgitate false statements. The idea of an "alternative fact" is an oxymoron. But there is an appropriate way to deal with questionable statements. Back in the day, a reporter might quote the statement that was purported to be untruthful or misleading, then cite an objective and highly authoritative source setting the record straight, in a way that a reader, listener, or viewer could see that it was false or misleading. But reporters never, ever should say that themselves. That is an opinion, a subjective judgment, not to be labeled as a fact, even if true.

Just as there is a role for news reporting, there is another for editorial writers and columnists, though, when a columnist also is a reporter, things get a bit problematic. For a time, there was widespread use by some news organizations of pieces clearly labeled "analysis" that straddled the line. But, by explicitly labeling an analysis, a caution flag warns that a piece is headed beyond the straightforward world of the four Ws. An editorial might accuse a public figure of saying things that are untrue or misleading, but it still is ill-advised to use the word "lie" or even "false." In a news story, those words and similar terms should not ever be used unless they are in a quote from someone else, another way of dealing with a prevarication. The key is that the conclusion must be drawn by the consumer of the reporting, not the purveyor.

It's fascinating to see where this lowering of journalistic standards is coming from. One doesn't have to be around long to notice how many journalists from major national news organizations have a tendency to look down their professional noses at those working on the local level. It also is not unknown for print journalists, particularly those at newspapers, to think of themselves as superior to their colleagues in television and radio (while often trying hard to get on the air themselves). And yet this lowering of standards is occurring almost exclusively on the national level and in print and digital outlets, not on broadcast television.

What is most painful is that two newspapers that I love and admire enormously, have read daily for almost a half-century, and pick up at the end of my driveway every morning are leading this downward spiral. The *New York Times,* where I first saw the word "lie" in a news story, and the *Washington Post,* which kept a count of what it recorded as Trump's false and misleading statements, have been the most aggressive in this effort to call Trump out. On the third anniversary of Trump taking the oath of office, the *Washington Post* reported that the president had made 16,241 false or misleading claims.

Could it be that the more combative nature of some national news organizations compared with their local counterparts has contributed to research findings that show national and local news media are seen differently? The Knight-Gallup study said, "Americans still believe local news outlets are doing many things right," and the study confirms that. Six in ten Americans believe local news organizations are accomplishing most of the key tasks of informing communities. And local journalists are seen as more caring, trustworthy, and neutral or unbiased.

To put a news organization so directly on the battle lines, in such a confrontational way, raises so many questions that one wonders if they were fully considered.

- What is the value of calling out the lie in an explicit way rather than showing that it was untrue in a less confrontational way?

- Is it worth the potential cost?

- What is the cost-benefit analysis of using the word?

- Is there really a need to make the media outlet the focus of the story rather than simply reporting the statement and putting authoritative evidence to the contrary next to it?

- How many *New York Times* readers would not have realized that Trump's remarks were a lie had the actual word not been used? Are *Times* readers not smart enough to draw that conclusion themselves?

- What is the standard for identifying a statement as a lie? Where is the red line?

- Will the new standard be uniformly applied?

- Would it have been applied to Hillary Clinton's statement that she had come under fire in Bosnia back in March 1996?

- What about Joe Biden's claim to have been arrested in South Africa in the 1970s?

Aren't these decisions highly subjective and problematic for a news organization?

When decisions like these are made, presumably at the editor level or even higher, was it considered that this would change a long-standing standard, one that would apply and have implications long after we are all gone? Is it worth it? My guess is that, in the future, such decisions will be looked back upon with considerable regret, a slippery slope, with no turning back.

While there has been some public discussion of what may well be the biggest change in the practice of journalism in a half-century or more, has it been enough? I think not nearly enough.

It is interesting that the charge into this previously uncharted journalistic territory was led by newspapers, long the most tradition-bound organizations. Characterizations such as "lie," "false," and "untrue" rarely are heard on the three major TV networks, which have played things more cautiously.

The world of cable is a mélange of actual reporting and information, opinion and attitude, with legitimate journalists and television personalities often sitting next to one another, with the ratio of reporting to opinion and attitude varying enormously from show to show.

More complicated and challenging are the roles played by those in print who both report and write columns as well for television journalists wearing multiple roles calling for both reporting and analyzing. For example, NBC News's Chuck Todd, moderator of *Meet the Press* and host of *MTP Daily* on MSNBC, also serves as NBC's political director and reports on news. Similarly, Andrea Mitchell, NBC's chief foreign-affairs reporter and senior Washington correspondent, hosts MSNBC's *Andrea Mitchell Reports* as well as reporting straight news. Both are required to step gingerly between the two roles and would be the first to admit that it's a tough straddle. (For more than two decades, I have had a contract with NBC News. I consider both Todd and Mitchell to be good and longtime friends and have nothing but the highest regard for each. They have tough jobs.)

Many in and outside of journalism have expressed concern about what they see as Trump's violation of norms in governance and behavior. But, in reaction, the top editors and executives of several of our most respected news organizations have, in my mind, violated longtime norms in journalism, already causing grave consequences.

With a large segment of Americans, this is a genie that never will go back into the bottle. Some might say that it is easy for me to throw rocks, having edited and published a political newsletter for thirty-eight years and having been a columnist for thirty-six years. I have not been a news reporter since my stint as a reporter (and photographer) for my junior and senior high-school newspapers. But that doesn't mean my concern for the profession is anything less.

Since I started my own publication in 1984, I have felt that we each have our brand, a reputation. Without a good reputation, little that we write, say, or do is of any real value. We in journalism have a serious problem, and implications for the future are ominous. I fear that great damage already has occurred and that every day the hole gets deeper. I fear that, long after Trump left office, the residual damage to the profession will be grave and possibly permanent.

CHARLIE COOK is the editor and publisher of the *Cook Political Report,* and a political analyst for the National Journal Group. Charlie is also a political analyst for NBC News. He is a member of the Board of Visitors of Louisiana State University's Manship School of Mass Communication.

THE GREATEST THREAT TO JOURNALISM'S FUTURE

TOM ROSENSTIEL

THE GREATEST THREAT to journalism's future is that Donald Trump will have goaded the press into becoming the institution he accuses it of being—a partisan opposition voice trying to persuade the public rather than inform it.

For journalism to survive, it must resist that temptation. When the current torrents of Trumpism and the collapse of the financial model of journalism have passed, journalism's future will depend on a handful of fundamental principles remaining. Key among them are fidelity to facts, to creating a public square where people can disagree, to a discipline of verification, separating reporting from opinion, and a commitment to dispassion and independence.

It is not guaranteed those principles will survive. Too many in journalism already are succumbing to seeing their role as opposing Trump, not reporting. One need look further only than what occurs a good deal of the time on cable-television news, particularly from the show hosts or so-called anchors. The biggest threat to journalism may be from within.

There are market pressures on the media to resort to a more partisan model: the more outlets we have competing, the more affirming an audience's viewpoint is a viable way to win trust. There are generational pressures inside newsrooms, as well, to call a lie by its name, not just provide people the facts of what was said or done and let audiences decide the implications and meaning of those facts for themselves. (The news is not hypodermic; the more journalists tell people what to think, the more skeptical audiences will resist and splinter.) There are also pressures on individual journalists to create their own identities online, to voice their personal views and build their own brands, that undermine the ability of journalistic institutions to claim independence in their coverage. There is the pressure of postmodernist arguments embraced by populists on the left and the right that the notions of independent fact-based reporting are a kind of delusion now exposed as fraudulent by the Internet.

We're also having an enormously healthy conversation within journalism to examine white-male-default culture in newsrooms. That conversation has also been connected to a simplistic and largely false definition of objectivity—the notion that a person can be wholly objective. The true and more sophisticated definition is that objectivity is a call for adopting more transparent, objective, and repeatable methods of reporting to make journalism more accurate and truthful. Understood this way—which was the way the term was intended when it migrated from social science—a default culture in newsrooms is a failure of objectivity and professional practice. It comes from denying that people bring their subjective experience to the news when in truth recognizing that is the first step to adopting an objective method.

And there is the president himself. Trump's approach to persuasion, his attitude toward facts, and his belief in how people come to understand the world around them are an existential challenge to the philosophical underpinnings of journalism.

Journalists by necessity arrive at understanding the world fact by fact. We report that these words were said. These actions occurred. This many people died. We build our version of journalistic truth—or what Bill Kovach and I in *The Elements of Journalism* call "functional truth"—from a sorting-out process of those facts over time. Each story, each account, is, as Carl Bernstein has called it, the best obtainable version of the truth up to that point. More facts over time add context. Eventually, through competing facts, more context, we will know enough of the story. Time is truth's ally. Speed and inattention are its enemies.

Trump and his political ascendance in America repudiated those philosophical foundations of modern journalism, which grew out of the Enlightenment and the notion that people with enough information, as rational beings, could govern themselves. When Trump as president was fact-checked false, his practice was to double-, triple-, and quadruple-down on the same falsehood, believing, apparently, that repetition can make people accept what had already been demonstrated to be untrue. Trumpism as it relates to journalism thus attacks not just the press. It attacks the empirical foundation upon which journalists have, perhaps too faithfully, built their profession.

To understand the depth of this challenge, it is worth examining some of Trump's rhetoric more closely. When he calls news "fake," it is a signal telling people to disbelieve any source but him. When he calls the press "the enemy of the people," he implies that any criticism of him really is a criticism of them for supporting him. And when he calls a news organization "failing," as he frequently described the *New York Times,* the underlying message is that the traditional media and their approach to fact-based independent reporting are on the wrong side of history—that his authoritarian view of reality, the leader as the sole source of truth and belief over facts as the best guide to knowledge, is the way of the future.

The rhetoric is crude but in its own way subtle and sophisticated. The challenge for the press is an existential one: How do you cover someone in a disinterested way who has called you the enemy? How do you maintain your professional discipline when someone has called you horrible and described work painstakingly done as fake?

It is no wonder that some journalists wonder why they should even try—or why, like Nancy Pelosi, they should not just tear up the speech.

I submit there are two overriding reasons that journalism as it navigates Trumpism should not take the bait—not become exactly what Trump accuses the press of being, a kind of opposition voice.

The first reason is immediate. The way to fact-check Trump or any populist using these techniques is to remain calm because that is what the audience requires of us. Imagine if you were a patient about to undergo surgery. Do you want the doctor to be nervous and tell you this is terrifyingly complicated surgery and she is anxious about it? Or do you want her to be calm, confident, and focused? Imagine you are in an encounter with law enforcement. Would you prefer the officer be calm? Or nervous, agitated, threatened, and angry? The analogy here is that we have a larger responsibility to the public than how we feel about what Trump has said or done today. Democracy depends on journalists being trusted observers on the public's behalf. To do that, we must leave behind some of our personal freedoms we might enjoy as any other member of the public.

The second reason journalists must rise above Trumpist goading is more long-term. How does journalism survive after Trump if it builds its audience and its economic model on the very divisions that Trump himself has built? How does journalism help to heal a divided country after he has gone? How do we persuade the public to trust us at that point if we abandon our principles of independence and calm authority now? How do we lay claim to being a public square if we were part of the partisan battle before? That is exactly what Trump wants.

Trump has set a trap for the press, one he refreshes day by day. The question is whether we jump at the red meat he has placed in that trap. Or do we have the professional discipline to resist, to do our jobs. Are we at war, as Marty Baron has put it, or at work? At the moment, I fear, journalism's greatest challenge is that it will destroy itself by taking the bait. Then where will that leave the press when Trump is gone?

TOM ROSENSTIEL is executive director of the American Press Institute, an applied think tank on media that describes itself "as a scout to the cavalry of the news industry looking to see what's coming next and building tools for it." He is the author of three novels and seven books of nonfiction, including, with Bill Kovach, *The Elements of Journalism: What News People Should Know and the Public Should Expect.*

III

THE STORY ISN'T ALWAYS IN WASHINGTON

FOR DECADES, scholars have told journalists to get out of Washington to uncover the issues that people really care about. The election of President Trump reminded journalists just how sage that advice is. Salena Zito of the *New York Post* and *Washington Examiner* writes about her refusal to use interstate highways, airplanes, and chain hotels when she is reporting. She opts for driving on back roads and staying at B&Bs and inns. Ginger Gibson, now at NBC News, shops Walmarts for interview subjects. Mark Ballard of the *Advocate* and *Times-Picayune* writes that the administration's relationships with the local press were better than with national media.

ALL POLITICAL JOURNALISM IS LOCAL—ESPECIALLY FOR TRUMP VOTERS

SALENA ZITO

HAD I BEGUN MY CAREER covering national politics in any place other than a medium-sized Pittsburgh newspaper—which had a healthy competition with another medium-sized Pittsburgh newspaper across the river—I am unsure I would have developed my style of covering elections.

The reporter who covered the same beat as mine for the competitor had a twenty-year jump on me with contacts and often spent his time on the press bus with presidential candidates and other reporters, giving him an edge on access and relationships.

My first (and last) time on a candidate's bus left me in tears. I felt cut off from the people who were actually going to—or not going to—vote for the candidate whose bus I was on. I also felt suffocated by the daily off-the-record propaganda that the campaign team fed all of us.

To me, every story coming out of that press bus was the same, because we all saw the same staged events and were given the same talking points.

I knew how the candidate felt about issues big and small. But I had no idea how the people felt about the candidate. So, I escaped from the bus when it was close to my home in Pennsylvania, called my boss and begged to be allowed to cover the elections from the viewpoint of the voters.

My boss's concern was whether my reporting could compete with our competitor's. My response was: Trust me.

He did. Since that moment, I have covered presidential and midterm elections from the places where the votes matter. If it is a midterm, then it is the swing districts in Pennsylvania, Wisconsin, North Carolina, Ohio, Colorado, Florida, and Michigan.

If it is a presidential election, it is in my home state of Pennsylvania as well as Wisconsin, Michigan, North Carolina, and Florida.

The first thing I do in preparation? Get out roadmaps, find where the local business clubs—Rotary, Elks, the doers of the community—meet. Then I learn about the high-school rivalries, where to get the best fish fry, which industries are growing and which are dying.

I never fly. I don't take interstates or turnpikes. I take only old US routes or state routes, and, yes, I often find bumpy dirt or gravel roads. But I can see how the cities and suburbs and counties change along the way. How they are prospering and growing, or decaying and failing.

I can pull over and talk to people on their porches or in the barber shops and in the mom-and-pop restaurants that are in almost every town.

I also almost always stay at a bed and breakfast or an inn. Why? Because their owners know what is going on, good and bad, in town.

To understand how I covered the Trump administration, step back to see how I got here. Covering the Pennsylvania and Ohio Republican primaries in spring 2016, I found that a new coalition was emerging among the GOP electorate that wasn't just the traditional mix of suburban country-club and evangelical voters (many of whom swung Democratic for Barack Obama). Blue-collar and labor voters were aligning with them, along with voters who rarely participated.

This coalition always was present in midterm and off-year elections since 2004 but never was as energized or engaged for Republican nominees John McCain and Mitt Romney. Donald Trump did not create this coalition; he is the result of it.

After the Pennsylvania primary ended and candidate Trump secured the Republican nomination, I found that the new coalition wasn't just a protest vote. It was the new Republican Party.

After both party conventions, I decided to drive around the sixty-seven counties of Pennsylvania and get a feel for what would happen in a state that has eluded the GOP since Bill Clinton won it in 1992.

What many people did not understand was that, since the 1996 reelection of Clinton over GOP nominee Bob Dole, the state became about 0.4 percentage points more Republican every four years.

So, in 1996, Clinton won twenty-eight of Pennsylvania's sixty-seven counties. By 2012, Barack Obama had won only thirteen. I wanted to see if this shift in coalitions was affecting counties that could take Trump over the finish line.

I pinpointed ten counties that were traditionally Democratic or weak Republican counties (when McCain and Romney did not inspire them enough to turn out) through interviews with voters and also the number of signs I saw.

The coauthor of our subsequent book, Brad Todd, would scold me and say, "Zito, signs don't vote." I understood that, but two things were different this time: the counties where the signs were in abundance and the intensity of those voters.

They didn't just go down to the local Republican headquarters and pick up campaign signs. In fact, the signs were more often than not homemade. I also saw barns and houses with Trump's name painted on the side. I even saw a horse with a Trump sign.

I understood then that, if those ten counties (which included Erie, Luzerne, Washington, Northampton, and Westmoreland) each had 2,000 more votes for Trump than Romney won in 2016, Trump would win. It did not matter if Hillary Clinton matched or exceeded what Barack Obama had done in the more populous Philadelphia "collar" counties. Those ten counties with those 2,000 extra voters each would give Trump Pennsylvania. And, if Pennsylvania was gone, then so were Ohio, Wisconsin, Michigan, North Carolina, and Florida. Why? Because Pennsylvania is five points more Democratic than those states. If Pennsylvania was gone, then so were those states.

I understood at that moment, based on my reporting as well as by following the weekly data coming out of the year-long Gallup analysis of 87,000 interviews of people about economic and social anxiety, that this election was likely over before anyone knew it.

Few understood that because, when they watched a rally on TV, they saw only the seven weirdest people in the crowd interviewed by nearly every network. The networks also showed only the seven goofiest things Trump said. There was plenty of material, but the viewer or reader was left with the impression that he couldn't win because he was odd and so were his supporters.

Those supporters instantly were branded as racist. In the Great Lakes and midwestern states, more than 20 percent of Trump supporters voted for Barack Obama twice, so this storyline—that they were dumb, old, and backward—infuriated them.

I found that, while economic anxiety and Trump's appeal were intertwined, a vote for Trump had much more to do with a community's setbacks, not voters' economic setbacks.

In fact, this coalition of supporters did not make lower-than-average wages if you subtract high-income areas such as New York, Washington, and Silicon Valley. These voters also were less likely to be unemployed.

Most were rooted in their communities, had been there for generations, and wanted their children and their grandchildren to stay in those communities. But opportunities were diminishing.

That sense of loss is profound. And the ridicule these voters received on the networks or social media was profound. They saw a culture that had diminishing respect for them, their ways of life, their work ethic, and their tendency to be rooted, not transient.

But few journalists spent time in their kitchens or neighborhoods or churches. Most reporters popped in for a day or two, staying at the Marriott by the airport to get their hotel points, and didn't get to know voters.

Despite covering elections from outside the press convoys, I still was able to interview every Republican and Democratic candidate running for president in 2016, from Lincoln Chafee to Hillary Clinton to George Pataki to Donald Trump.

In September 2016, my Pittsburgh newspaper downsized. I took the buyout. As I was walking out of my beloved newspaper (and crying), I received a text from Trump's Pennsylvania campaign asking if I wanted to interview the nominee the next day. I said yes in my outside voice. In my inside voice, I freaked out because I didn't have a job.

After several calls to major newspapers about the interview, I agreed to write about it for *The Atlantic*. In the interview, two things happened: I saw up close and personal how Trump related to the people behind the scenes of the conference where he was speaking—the electricians, laborers, service workers—rather than the elites who attended the conference.

Editors took notice when I quoted Todd's observation about Trump that "voters take you seriously, but not literally. And my profession takes everything you say literally but does not take your candidacy seriously."

In the next six weeks, I worked for four news organizations, writing four different stories every day, seven days a week, while driving across the country. On election night 2016, I watched my ten counties come in, all above the 2,000 number that was needed to swing Pennsylvania. I understood before 9 p.m. that the election was over.

Several things have happened since then: The *New York Post* kept me on as a weekly columnist, the *Washington Examiner* hired me as a staff reporter and columnist, and CNN hired me as a contributor. I coauthored *The Great Revolt: Inside the Populist Coalition Reshaping American Politics,* I taught at Harvard and Washington and Lee, leaving the campuses to get to know the people living around them. I also wrote for the *Wall Street Journal.*

I have interviewed the president twice since he was sworn in, first in the Oval Office and then in the basement of a hockey arena in Erie, Pennsylvania. I have interviewed the secretaries of transportation, state, defense, energy, education, housing and urban development, and Vice President Mike Pence.

Of the White Houses I have covered, from George W. Bush through Barack Obama to Donald Trump, this one has been the most accessible. It also is the most different. The president bypassed my profession by using social media, often several times a day, and he did "gaggles" at Marine One, sometimes daily.

As a reporter still doing the same thing I always have done, I will say that nothing has changed in terms of support for President Trump. Very few have left his coalition. In my reporting in Wisconsin, Michigan, Ohio, and Pennsylvania, I heard anecdotal examples of how he was winning over people who were unsure about him in 2016.

The underreported and misreported segment of our country is not the White House. It is the people, their lives and their stories outside of the stereotypes that my profession likes to tag them with. As long as we keep looking for a story an editor tells us to get, rather than the story that is happening, we will struggle to understand our whole country.

SALENA ZITO writes for the *New York Post* and the *Washington Examiner.* She is a contributor to CNN and coauthored *The Great Revolt: Inside the Populist Coalition Reshaping American Politics.*

SHOPPING FOR TRUMP VOTERS AT WALMART

GINGER GIBSON

A WALMART IN A SUBURB outside Cincinnati, Ohio, was the backdrop for the moment when I realized just how much being branded "the fake news" was hampering me in doing my job.

The location had been picked with great consideration. It was October 2018 and, as the leaves were turning and the air was getting crisp in Ohio, voters were weeks away from deciding who should represent them in Congress. The election was being cast as a referendum on President Donald Trump, but the number-one rule of elections is that all politics are local. There was no doubt it would be the same here.

This district resembled an attempt by a preschooler to draw a block-letter V, gerrymandered in a way to balance the suburbs-to-urban ratio and ensure that the seat remained safely in Republican hands.

Republican Steve Chabot was elected to Congress in 1994 and, other than two years when he was bounced from the chamber before being quickly returned, he was running again to represent the area.

Republicans knew it was a tough race. Chabot faced a formidable opponent at a time when Democrats were making gains across the country. But Chabot represented the potential for something Republicans were scrambling to find—the Democratic blue-wave high mark. His party was banking that, when the tide of Democratic victories rolled over, Chabot would be standing.

I went to Ohio to chronicle the race, a national reporter who had eaten at a Skyline Chili before and dipped in and out of the district while following presidential campaigns. But I had no deep understanding of what it was like to live in the area. I had grown up in the South, surrounded by rice and sugar fields and oil refineries. Rural America wasn't foreign to me, but suburban Ohio was just as distinct from my native Gulf Coast as France.

I knew I would find reliably Republican voters at this Walmart, in the northeastern part of the district. Democrats were banking that suburban voters had grown weary of Trump, that, after two years of tweeting and shouting and scandal and Russia, voters would punish his party instead of rewarding it for a booming economy. Republicans were hoping that delivering a tax cut and watching a growing stock market would be enough to beat back the national angst about Trump's tone. And candidates such as Chabot—who once had lost reelection on a national wave—were being proactive about fending off the challenge.

All of that was spin and strategy and hypothesizing. Campaigns and their political committees in Washington spend gobs of money on polling and focus groups to inform that strategy and spin. But hearing the parties give you their best case isn't the same as hearing it from voters.

Walmart parking lots have become my one-woman focus groups. Sometimes I opt for a Target or a Whole Foods or a Wegmans or a Meijer. Lots of reporters prefer coffee shops and diners: Your targets are seated and it's harder for them to get away. But a Walmart almost always is perfect. Walmart shoppers aren't of a singular economic background. They work a myriad of jobs. And their political views run the gamut. I estimated in 2016 that I spent more than fifty hours in Walmart parking lots talking to voters. I wish I could tell you that it helped me predict Trump's win. It didn't, but it made me less surprised when he was declared victorious.

On that October in Ohio, I was looking for Trump voters who were considering going either way in the midterm election. I wanted to know whether the president's recent trip there had swayed minds. I wanted to know if they were tired of him. I wanted to know if they still adored him.

A man in a zip-up vest and a ball cap emerged pushing a half-empty cart.

"Hello! Good afternoon," I began, using a chipper voice I had mastered in my first job, working at a McDonald's. I was certain most people thought the young-looking woman in jeans with a smile was trying to sell something, but my demeanor usually got their attention.

"My name is Ginger and I'm a reporter from Washington and I was just wondering if I could bother you for a couple of minutes while you walk to your car and unload your groceries" was generally enough to know whether you were going to get an interview. Their facial expression said it first.

The man, who appeared to be in his forties or fifties, turned to me quickly.

"Fake news!" he shouted. "You're nothing but fake news. You just want to hurt our president. You're fake news. I know how you work."

He became so animated that he forgot about his cart. He turned to me and pointed, continuing to rant: "America would be better off without the mainstream media."

I stood frozen. Listening to him shout, not wanting to further inflame him. And then watching over his shoulder as his cart continued to roll. It was now ten yards away from him. It crashed into a parked car.

"Your cart, sir," I said as he turned around. "Thank you anyway. Have a nice day."

The episode almost was comical, a scene out of a bad comedy that only people who obsessively follow political news would find funny.

But it was illuminating at the same time. I had traveled five hundred miles to hear the opinions of shoppers like him. I wanted to know what he liked about Trump. I wanted him to inform my readers. He clearly was an impassioned fan of the president, and his perspective was important. And I couldn't get it. A guy who was so enraged by the current conditions—of the world or the press or the president—would not be part of my story.

He wasn't the first stranger to dismiss me rudely in a parking lot, nor the last. In the era of Trump, reporters have hit a unique stumbling block: The people we need to be talking to the most are being told not to talk to us. It makes our jobs harder but not impossible.

Trump rails against the press, an apparent effort to undermine anything we may publish or broadcast that he feels could damage his brand. It's a double-edged sword. He has convinced the people who adore him the most to not trust us, to be actively hostile to us. And that deprives coverage of his presidency of the voices that would sing his praise.

Change never happens on a single track, and a confluence of factors is contributing to political reporters' isolation from the people we need most to do our jobs: voters. Local news organizations are shrinking. Resources for reporters to travel the country are diminishing. Instead, we're replacing our exposure with the echo chamber of Twitter and other social media. But the man shouting in a parking lot in Mason, Ohio, is different from the one shouting behind the veil of anonymity on Twitter.

We need to be talking to people. That nameless man wasn't the only one who has taught me a good deal about doing my job in the era of Trump.

On the day when Dr. Christine Blasey Ford told the US Senate that, as a teenager, she had been assaulted by Supreme Court nominee Brett Kavanaugh, I called women across the country. (I obtained their phone numbers from a poll.) Three answered their phones. The hearing was on in the background. That crystallized for me that this story wasn't just a Washington phenomenon.

I traveled to Maine in the days before the impeachment proceedings. On Main Street in the formerly industrial city of Lewiston, a man who once favored the president explained how his mind had been changed about the president.

It was an Uber driver in Charleston, South Carolina, who told me she voted for Trump but wanted him just to stop tweeting, joining a chorus I heard at nearly every turn.

And it was a pair of women at a barbecue restaurant, where I was eating dinner, outside of Milwaukee who offered the best insight into the Democratic presidential primary: They just wanted to see an end to the chaos.

All of these incidents are anecdotal. But each voter I spoke with reminds me of his or her importance. No poll or focus group can replace the face-to-face interactions that journalists need. As Trump continues to work to undermine our ability to have those discussions, it is critical that we work even harder.

GINGER GIBSON was a political reporter based in Washington for Reuters. She now is a digital politics editor at NBC. She is a graduate of Louisiana State University's Manship School.

RELATIONS ARE BETTER OUTSIDE OF WASHINGTON

MARK BALLARD

A LITTLE MORE THAN A MONTH after Donald Trump rode down an escalator to announce his candidacy in June 2015, he gave his first interview in Louisiana. Broadcast statewide for decades, Moon Griffon's talk-radio show has been a Louisiana Republican megaphone, relying on angry "us" versus "them" rhetoric to energize the conservative base to an increasingly partisan agenda.

Guest hosting that day was Jeff Landry, then a candidate in what would be a successful race for state attorney general. Landry had ridden the Tea Party insurgency to a term in Congress only to be unseated when the state's loss of population forced the loss of a congressional seat.

Under Landry's gentle probing, Trump said, "I'm not controlled by lobbyists and special interests and donors. . . . I'm not controlled by anybody." On his third trip to Louisiana as president, visiting the Cameron Liquefied Natural Gas plant in Hackberry, near Lake Charles, in May 2019, Trump said, "Louisiana, a state I love very much and based on the votes I should love it."

Trump won the state with 58 percent of the vote in the 2016 presidential election, receiving more votes than any previous candidate on a Louisiana ballot. He remains popular in a state where Republicans dominate both chambers of the legislature, all but one of the eight US House and Senate seats, and all but one of the officials elected statewide. With six trips to Louisiana—five in 2019 alone—Trump has visited the state more than any other president in history—and that doesn't count the trips he made as a candidate.

All of which has left many scratching their heads. Louisiana has only eight electoral votes, with little chance that they'll go to anyone else. Seven of the eight congressmen have voiced devotion to Trump and his agenda. And, while his visits have been widely covered locally, Trump has had little direct interaction with the local media—none with print reporters. A reality-show star who understands politics as entertainment, Trump is a master of dominating the "earned-media" scene, using tweets, often with outrageous messages, that dominate coverage during an era when largely depopulated newsrooms are required to fill far larger spaces, faster, on a 24/7 pace. He doesn't need to answer reporters' questions to get his narrative into the national dialogue.

"I think the media have a distorted image of who he actually is," Landry told the *Advocate*. "If you bring the president to a place like a restaurant, he will talk to the waiters, the cooks, everyone there. He loves working people."

That approach fits right in to the wheelhouse of Louisiana voters. Louisiana was the first state that wasn't previously ruled by England to join the union. Its voters long have loved self-confident rakes who rule with a hint of authoritarianism.

They like their politics to be entertaining and flavored with populist rhetoric. Think David Duke, a Ku Klux Klan leader who was nearly elected to the US Senate and ran as a Republican for governor in the early 1990s. Or Edwin W. Edwards, who was elected governor four times despite constantly being under federal investigation, the last of which sent him to prison.

Think Huey Long, who attacked special interests on behalf of the common folk. When applying in 1978 to put the thirty-four-story state capitol, which Long built in the early 1930s, on the National Register of Historic Places, the application described Long as having a "political style and tactics of polemical attack, personalized invective, guilt by association, and the unfounded accusation displayed a demagogic streak. . . . Above all he gave the 'common man' the psychological feeling that he represented him and that the traditional elite no longer ran the state for its benefit."

It's a description that fits Trump. In his first major campaign appearance in February 2016, Trump didn't speak with the media, but *Times-*

Picayune reporter Richard Rainey described his speech to a Baton Rouge crowd of about 10,000 as "barroom bravado and sentences lacking subjects, he presented one scapegoat after another, and the audience loved it."

As a presidential candidate, Trump became the first national figure to visit Louisiana after more than twenty inches of rain flooded thousands of homes and businesses and killed thirteen. The August 2016 flooding had gone largely unnoticed nationally until Trump's visit, which was made over the objections of local law-enforcement officials, who didn't want to be diverted with candidate-safety concerns while they still were rescuing people from their homes.

Trump was widely photographed waving to flood victims, who asked for his autograph, and the coverage attracted national attention. The closest a reporter got to the candidate was when a firefighter let an *Advocate* reporter into a private meeting at the makeshift St. Amant operations center south of Baton Rouge on the condition the reporter keep quiet and not identify himself. Trump praised first responders in that crowded room, then went out to be photographed unloading supplies.

In his trips to New Orleans and Baton Rouge as president, Barack Obama came to support programs rather than campaign. His trips were official and, though local reporters were allowed to join the motorcade, they were kept at a distance. However, Obama always made a point to speak to them directly.

Still, voters learned that Obama got an earful about Baton Rouge's traffic problems only when Mayor Kip Holden complained publicly that it was he, not Governor John Bel Edwards, who brought the issue to the president's attention.

In that way, Trump acts similarly. Local interviews are short and rarely go beyond advertising his accomplishments. Local reporters could ask about impacts national programs have on Louisiana, but the interviews are only a few minutes long, not enough time for follow-up questions.

Anchor Jeff Hochak of KNOE-TV in Monroe tried to hit several topics during a short interview prior to Trump's Nov. 6, 2019, rally for GOP gubernatorial candidate Eddie Rispone.

Hochak hit on trade with China—the trade war had hurt Louisiana farmers—but he also had to ask about the campaign rally as well as the upcoming LSU-Alabama football game, which Trump was attending. Hochak also asked about the effectiveness of a dozen US Immigration and Customs Enforcement detention centers in Louisiana. ICE was shipping those stopped at the Texas border without proper documents to Louisiana.

"Oh, yeah, you don't want those people around you, I'll tell you what. And ICE has done an incredible job and these are stone-cold killers," Trump said. The interview soon ended, and the president walked off.

The Monroe rally was the second of three events Trump held in Louisiana in hopes that his popularity would rub off and unseat John Bel Edwards, the only Democratic governor in the otherwise ruby-red Deep South. A seventy-year-old Baton Rouge businessman, Rispone had been a big donor to GOP causes but was largely unknown to the electorate. He spent about $12 million of his money, most on television commercials that promoted Trump as much as himself.

Trump tried to tie Edwards to national Democratic positions that the governor didn't hold. Edwards is against abortion and for gun rights. "Right now, Louisiana can send the radical left a message they can never ignore," Trump said, asking the cheering crowd to fire Edwards. "Eddie will defend your values that are under assault by the extreme left."

Trump didn't rein in his rhetoric, claiming Edwards was against gun ownership and was responsible for the state's devasting economy. Minutes before these statements, Trump's White House released a statement saying Louisiana had a great economy with a growing number of jobs. And, unlike Trump, Edwards is an avid hunter who owns a lot of guns and has since he was a child. The incongruity made no impression on the crowd, which jeered Edwards as a quixotic liberal hoping to turn the country socialist. Unlike official visits, where the press is vetted and kept on a short leash by the Secret Service, campaign rallies are unofficial and a lot laxer. Sam Karlin, a reporter for the *Advocate,* the state's largest newspaper, recalls arriving at Monroe to receive his credentials. The media table was staffed by state party officials who knew Karlin and didn't ask for picture identification, as required.

Karlin wandered around the arena, talking with audience members, whom he didn't know, and public officials, whom he did. About an hour before the event was scheduled to begin, the press was corralled into a pen in the middle of the arena.

When Trump spoke, he blasted the media as biased liars, evoking boos and sneers, often angry, directed at the reporters' pen.

Karlin knew that Trump's invective was aimed at the national media but was unsure if a hostile crowd could or would make such distinctions. "I remember looking around to see where the police were standing," he recalled.

After the event, as the national media headed back to Air Force One with Trump, Karlin recalled how members of the audience used their smart phones to videotape the local reporters hustling to meet deadlines. Some shouted threats.

Trump made his third election-cycle trip on November 18, this time to Bossier City in northwest Louisiana. He called Democrats "sinister" and "deranged," while dubbing the impeachment hearings a "witch hunt."

Through the rest of the campaign, Edwards stayed focused on how he led a reversal of years of budget deficits into a surplus that allowed the state to spend more money, for the first time in more than decade, on education. Edwards never attacked the popular president. When asked about Trump's comments, he responded with stories about his nine visits to the White House.

But Trump's visits to Louisiana had energized the president's opponents to get out and vote. Edwards won the runoff against Rispone by 40,000 votes of 1.5 million cast.

During a visit to Louisiana, on Jan. 13, 2020, to attend the National College Football Championship game, he gave a short interview to Katie Moore, of WWL-TV in New Orleans.

Edwards had been inaugurated to a second term earlier in the day, so naturally Moore asked about Trump's view of the Democratic governor. Trump said Edwards, who also was at the game, had come up to shake his hand. "He was terrific," Trump said.

Trump had campaigned in all three of the 2019 gubernatorial races— all in Republican-majority states. Democrats beat Republicans in two contests and came very close to winning the third. Trump was nonplussed, noting that he bolstered Rispone's performance. "And John Bel's a pro and we're going to work together; we're going to do everything we can for the state."

Trump left the interview and walked out onto the field of the New Orleans Superdome to thunderous applause.

MARK BALLARD is editor of the capitol bureau of the *Advocate*, for which he reports and writes a column.

IV

COVERING THE PRESIDENT WHEN YOU'RE A JOURNALIST OF COLOR

MARY C. CURTIS of *Roll Call* and Jesse J. Holland, formerly of the Associated Press, say that the hard-won respect for Black journalists diminished during the Trump era. Fernando Pizarro, formerly of Univision, contends that the administration didn't really care about Spanish-language media. But "Fin" Gomez of CBS News tells how he lived out his dream as a producer in Washington.

JOURNALISM IN THE TRUMP ERA IS NO FUN WHEN THERE'S A TARGET ON YOUR BACK

MARY C. CURTIS

EARLY IN MY CAREER, I walked, wrote, and edited on eggshells. Ever under the microscope and, as an African American woman, in the minority in any newsroom, I sometimes was questioned on how my upbringing and identity would affect my work. And usually that examination was framed as a negative. As my bosses told me I was hired to bring a different perspective to the job, I got the very clear message that success meant fitting in—with them. "We love you just the way you are. Now, change."

This was ironic, as I had entered the profession, in part, because growing up in a family of readers and thinkers, activists and contrarians in a working-class and close-knit Black neighborhood in West Baltimore, I had recognized the disconnect in the lives we led and the way we were portrayed in newspapers and on broadcast news shows.

Still, I enjoyed testing myself, going outside my comfort zone, and proving each time I could enter into worlds my editors and I never would have expected. I made the rounds, covering the first national Tea Party gathering in Opryland, winning a Thomas Wolfe Award for an examination of Confederate heritage groups.

That story took me to meetings that began with a rebel yell, where Lincoln was derided as a war criminal who deserved his fate, and where the Stars and Bars replaced the Stars and Stripes when attendees swore allegiance.

I used my difference, sitting down for breakfast or drinks with people who were so busy proving they weren't motivated by racism that they were kind to me while calling President Barack Obama a Marxist and worse.

It became my trademark. I took it in, and took it, in more ways than one. But at a cost many of my white colleagues did not have to pay.

The Trump presidency made that clear. When President Trump ranted, rambled, and went on the attack, it was nothing if not dramatic. Does good drama make for good journalism? The answer seemed to be an uneasy but definite "yes" during candidate Donald Trump's 2016 run for the presidency. As then-CBS executive Leslie Moonves said: "It may not be good for America, but it's damn good for CBS."

In a speech at a tech conference, Moonves called the campaign a "circus" full of "bomb throwing," and said he hoped it would continue, according to the *Hollywood Reporter*. "Man, who would have expected the ride we're all having right now? . . . The money's rolling in and this is fun," he said, salivating at the bottom-line gold to be had from political advertising.

As networks covered Trump rallies start to finish, it was a political and journalism decision, as well, news judgment skewed to favor one candidate with valuable free airtime because of . . . ratings? Trump always has had a love/hate relationship with the media that predated his presidential curses against "the enemy of the people." In his New York City days as a real-estate guy and man-about-town, Trump would call the tabloids, under an assumed name, to report on his exploits.

That his antics could incite or hurt real people was seldom a consideration, because the gatekeepers weren't the ones being singed by his scorched-earth approach. Trump's background did not disqualify him from being a TV entertainer and eventually the president of the United States.

The reality—not the reality show—presented a dilemma for journalists. Though burned repeatedly throughout the Trump years, the media have tried to adhere to a tradition Trump ignored. For a group of supposedly astute professionals, it could be seen as malpractice.

How do folks in the media, and media organizations, deal with the rule breaker in the White House? Evidence shows that, for the most part, they have not figured it out.

Look at it this way: The lion tamer at any "circus" often gets eaten in the end. On one side, charges of "alternative facts," "fake-news" pundits at one major network, and a flurry of conservative radio shows and Internet blogs that act as GOP and Trump allies. On the other, journalists trying to stick to a standard of objectivity, when I'm increasingly convinced there never has been any such thing.

Let me explain how it looked to someone who always has been an outsider. Many of my fellow journalists were as mesmerized as Moonves, who, interestingly, was forced out of his job (with an attendant golden parachute) after charges of sexual harassment, as the president, with his own list of similar charges, continued to command the airwaves on his terms.

Perhaps those assigned to keep track of Trump struggled to cover the outrageousness of some of his statements. Maybe they bent over backward to give the president the benefit of the doubt. They kept waiting, waiting, waiting for the presidency to elevate the man, and for the White House to follow protocol, even as formal press briefings morphed from hostile to nonexistent. Maybe a few got caught up in the emotion and electricity that coursed through the crowd at a Trump rally.

It was surprising to witness—but then it wasn't for someone who, unlike many of my colleagues, never expected fairness or equality in the media or in the world.

Never had I felt so vulnerable as I had at any Trump rally. He was not a Tea Party protester, or a stalwart dressed in Confederate gray, eager to talk, talk with and, let's face it, dismiss. He was the most powerful person in the world, leading a crowd whose individual members—teachers, doctors, mechanics—could be perfectly polite while offering the occasionally provocative quote but then turn on a dime to fill an arena with chants of "lock her up" or "build the wall."

I admit I always was more comfortable as a member of the crowd roaming through the arena invisible, interrupted occasionally by a Trump fan, complimenting me for being a Black person not on the "Democrat plantation."

When the president trained laser-focused attacks on the press pen, colleagues who are not Black or brown were covered in a sort of camouflage as I was laid bare. Among the protesters Trump insulted, those of color seemed to come in for particularly harsh treatment, jostled and taunted, and in a memorable rally in Fayetteville, North Carolina, sucker-punched. It was frightening, and personal.

With this president, it often was personal, his words and actions affecting me, my relatives, people I love, the complex and fascinating residents of West Baltimore, who taught me so much. When Trump called my hometown a "disgusting, rat- and rodent-infested mess," as a columnist I could report it and comment on it. I imagined a child growing up there, as I did, waking up to Trump's tweet that "no human being would want to live there."

Though reporting bolsters my columns, I also get to reveal a bit of myself, facts and insights that might not have occurred to many of my readers—or at least that's what the nice ones tell me.

In truth, though, everyone brings that background with them, and it can't help but be reflected in the coverage, whether or not it is tagged opinion.

Those days in the newsroom were sometimes lonely because of judgments that revealed their own biases, from colleagues as well as supervisors. It's not as though journalists leave their backgrounds or preconceived notions at the front door, no matter how much they believe they do.

When they learned where I came from, more than a few had views not that dissimilar from the president's. Those who respected me often saw me as a unicorn, an exception who escaped from a neighborhood that was, yes, a dystopian hellhole. Actually, those years gave me advantages—and sources—that made me a better journalist and, I and my late parents hoped and prayed, a better person.

I could see how my coworkers' own childhoods, education, and worldviews affected how they covered city workers, poor people, people who needed food assistance, felons, the disenfranchised in stories labeled "news." It's something I no longer can ignore when unfiltered attacks that seem plain as day are described as "racially charged" or "racially tinged," whatever that means, for the sake of "objectivity."

Do colleagues without skin in the game take a moment to consider that the journalists who have someone undocumented in their families, who have sons and daughters who have been profiled, or relatives who have been caught in an often-unjust criminal-justice system might take longer at the end of the day to wash it all off, if they ever can? It's hard to seek objectivity when there is a target on your back.

This president and his administration called out media bias daily. And while great journalists continue to investigate, to report and reveal facts behind the Trumpian stone wall, there were stories that don't get told enough, with enough depth and compassion. That's the bias I see.

Trump has his supporters among minorities, who are not monolithic as voters or people. But, when many American citizens of color talk to me about their fear when they hear "Make America Great Again," because the idea of going back is too terrible to contemplate, they look into my eyes, believing I can understand. On some level, I do.

That some journalists can afford to keep a distance from the biggest story of our time, the way the Trump years have changed the notion of America and Americans, is a fact.

The Trump presidency revealed that the notion of objectivity in journalism is elusive and nearly impossible to achieve, that "neutral" and "fair" mean different things to different people, which means, as I have long suspected, it has revealed nothing new at all.

MARY C. CURTIS is a columnist for *Roll Call*, the Capitol Hill news organization, and a contributor to WCCB-TV and WFAE, a National Public Radio station, in Charlotte, North Carolina. She is a senior facilitator with the OpEd Project, which tries to increase the range of voices in opinion writing, and has worked at the *New York Times, Charlotte Observer,* the *Sun* in Baltimore, and the Associated Press.

SOMETHING CHANGED FOR BLACK JOURNALISTS AFTER TRUMP WAS ELECTED

JESSE HOLLAND

FOR A BRIEF, SHINING MOMENT, it seemed we had overcome. President Barack Obama's election seemed to usher in a new day of respect not just for Black America but for the African American media, and African Americans in media. Just as the president wasn't the Black president—but THE president—African Americans seemed to be elevated in the industry from being just Black journalists to JOURNALISTS, seen finally as equal to our colleagues.

At last, our skills, drives, ambitions, interests, and storytelling skills were being acknowledged and appreciated as being equivalent to those of our colleagues.

Despite being only 7 percent of newsrooms, according to the Pew Research Center, we had the respect and opportunities that long had been denied us in the mainstream media despite our talents and hard work: Lester Holt sat atop the *NBC Nightly News*, and Dean Baquet ruled the *New York Times*. *Code/Switch* was one of National Public Radio's most popular programs, and race and ethnicity coverage—long the least-funded, sometimes-disrespected, and often rarely appreciated outside of hackneyed stories about crime, ghettos, and poverty—flourished at news organizations in a way not seen since the civil-rights movement, reinvigorating and opening eyes to the work of those once sneered at by their colleagues and the public as "race writers."

We were able to explain the changing world—our world—in a way our colleagues couldn't, didn't, and hadn't—and people finally paid attention. As Samuel Cornish and John B. Russwurm, founders of *Freedom's*

Journal, the nation's first Black newspaper, proclaimed In 1827: "We wish to plead our own cause. Too long have others spoken for us."

They listened as we talked about the contributions of African American slaves not only to the White House and the Capitol but to the United States in general and the South in particular. They listened as we talked about genealogy, sociology, psychology, and the long-term and still-ongoing impacts of American slavery, the failed Reconstruction efforts, and Jim Crow. Their eyes were opened to the horrors of Red Summer, the continuing disrespectful sexism focused at African American women, the school-to-prison pipeline aimed at African American boys, and the ongoing struggle to deal with the repercussions of, and the lack of trust engendered by, historically uncaring and sometimes blatantly racist police policies around the United States.

Across the mediums, African American journalists finally had the respect our predecessors were due but never fully received. Finally, our voices were heard.

President Trump was elected. And something changed. Despite years of struggles and proving that we were more than just a monolith, that we were more than just our race, that we deserved everything we had achieved, that the stories we had to tell were worth hearing, all of a sudden we were just Black journalists again.

Yes, some of the advances were still there, some of the achievements stayed, but the respect for our hard-won professionalism and objectivity seemed to erode a little bit every day in the public mind, encouraged by snide and dismissive remarks from the new administration.

True or not, it seemed as if the ire and ardor that the Trump administration focused on all nonconservative media was magnified against African American journalists—especially Black women working as journalists on the White House beat.

Snide behind-the-scenes attacks burst into the public the day that the president asked American Urban Radio Network's April Ryan if she could set up a meeting for him with the Congressional Black Caucus.

"Are they friends of yours?" the president asked her.

Because, of course, all Black people know each other and are friends. Because, of course, a Black journalist would have an "in" with the almost completely Democratic Congressional Black Caucus. Because, of course, Ryan, a Black woman working at the White House, should have been willing to do secretarial-like work, even though she's a longtime award-winning White House reporter and political analyst.

But that tone-deaf statement soon was joined by other pointed attacks on Black journalists at the White House. Trump later attacked Ryan again, calling her a "loser" who "doesn't know what the hell she is doing."

The administration's disrespect soon expanded beyond Ryan. When asked by CNN White House correspondent Abby Phillip whether his acting attorney general should "rein in" special counsel Robert Mueller, who at the time was investigating the administration, Trump refused to answer the question and instead insulted Phillip.

"What a stupid question that is," he said, wagging his finger at a grown woman trying to do her job. "What a stupid question."

And, when Phillip tried to respond, Trump talked right over her with another insult. "I watch you a lot, you ask a lot of stupid questions."

And when PBS NewsHour's Yamiche Alcindor asked Trump about the implications of calling himself a nationalist in a country where white nationalists often are considered to be racists, Trump, instead of answering or explaining himself, instead went on the attack again, accusing Alcindor of asking "a racist question."

With each insult, the administration's rancor toward Black journalists was picked up by the public and allowed it to feel free to stereotype African American journalists again.

Ryan had to hire herself a bodyguard. Phillip and Alcindor, instead of doing their jobs, had to spend time defending their reputations as journalists.

While we are not a monolith—Black journalists are found at Fox News as well as MSNBC, at the Wall Street Journal as well as at the New York Times—we all have the same story to tell when it comes to being singled out because of our race and culture. And Black journalists found themselves in the crosshairs.

While no longer actively covering the White House, the Supreme Court, Congress, or politics, I noticed an increase in vitriolic, offensive e-mail from readers and viewers when I worked at the Associated Press and C-SPAN. Like many others, I've received so many e-mails calling me a "nigger," a "coon," and other racial epithets that I stopped saving or even noticing them.

But it's not always the vicious ones who hurt. I always will remember the reader who was surprised to meet me in person: "I always thought you were white," he exclaimed. "You don't write Black."

Other African American journalists reported the same, sometimes in quiet conversations with colleagues and sometimes publicly. But it seems to be getting worse.

In February 2020, the FBI arrested four "racially motivated violent extremists" from four states for delivering threats to journalists of color and others via posters that included statements like "Your Actions Have Consequences" and "You have been visited by your local Nazis," with disturbing imagery and the name and address of the recipient.

While threats against American journalists seem to be on the rise overall, it is more concerning with African American journalists, given this country's history of violence against Black journalists.

Black journalists have faced white violence since their inception, going back to the burning of Ida B. Wells's newspaper, the *Free Speech and Headlight*, in 1892 in Memphis, Tennessee, for reporting on lynching in the South and the destruction of the *Wilmington Daily Record* in Wilmington, North Carolina, in 1898 for denouncing the myth that African American men were raping white women.

Black journalists face a more present danger given this country's history—but that never has stopped us. Nelson Mandela once said, "Education is the most powerful weapon we can use to change the world." Like Wells and the legions of Black journalists who preceded us, we will ignore the venomous and malicious taunts from presidential administrations and mobs alike, from the trolls on Twitter and the letter writers, from our detractors and our opponents, and continue to do the work that is needed to allow this country to achieve the hopes of our ancestors.

JESSE HOLLAND is a former race and ethnicity reporter for the Associated Press, where he also covered the White House, Supreme Court, and Congress. He frequently appears on C-SPAN. He is a distinguished visiting scholar in residence at the John W. Kluge Center at the Library of Congress, where he researches African American history in the Washington area. He is the author or coauthor of four books, including *The Invisibles: The Untold Story of African American Slaves in the White House.*

COVERING *EL GOBIERNO DE TRUMP Y LA CASA BLANCA*

A Different Take

FERNANDO PIZARRO

SURELY EVERY POLITICAL REPORTER in the country remembers June 16, 2015, when Donald Trump came down the escalator in his namesake tower in Manhattan and announced his candidacy for the White House. Certainly, almost everyone recalls his words about Mexico not sending its "best people" and, in fact, sending many "rapists." Fewer people may remember that, two months later, Trump kicked one of Univision's main news anchors, Jorge Ramos, out of a campaign press conference in Dubuque, Iowa.

Compared with previous presidential campaigns, it was a rocky and inauspicious start to the relationship between what would become the Trump administration and Univision in particular, and Spanish-language media in general.

Securing an exclusive, one-on-one interview or even a quote from a Cabinet secretary, high-ranking official, or spokesperson is essential to any story about an administration and its policies, no matter the language in which it is reported. Logistics get more complicated when it must be on-camera. All of the efforts are worthwhile if the interview generates headlines or simply adds an official reaction to solid reporting.

However, if that interview is to be held *en español,* with someone who is fluent, then the level of complexity must be multiplied by two or three. Categorized or even sidelined as specialty or ethnic media by recent administrations, Spanish-language outlets in the United States nonetheless serve an audience of more than 58 million Hispanics, a not-soinsignificant share of the population and the second largest racial or ethnic group in the country, according to the Pew Research Center.

Sometimes favored when an administration wants to get a message across, on other occasions Spanish-language media get the short end of the stick, as they are not given scoops or priority.

While recent studies have dissected the number of Hispanics who consume news in Spanish or English, or in both languages, the fact is that Spanish-language outlets cover topics that the English-language mainstream media often do not. They frequently break news that English-language mainstream outlets miss, mainly because of the language barrier or simply a lack of interest.

In the last three decades, administrations increasingly have recognized that and have strived to provide Hispanic media with access to high-ranking officials and spokespeople at the White House and federal agencies. The Trump administration did not completely reverse this trend, but its record was mixed.

Even though there was almost zero outreach by the Trump campaign during the 2015–16 primary season, it was the Republican National Committee media team who picked up the slack regarding Spanish-language coverage. As the primary season drew to a close, the RNC lost a few Hispanic media staffers who did not want to be spokespeople for then-candidate Trump.

By the Republican Convention in Cleveland in the summer of 2016, Helen Aguirre Ferré, a veteran journalist, host, and political analyst with GOP ties in South Florida, surprised many in her own party by taking the job of RNC Hispanic spokesperson. She had been an adviser for the Jeb Bush presidential campaign. Aided by other seasoned Republican operatives, some of them veterans of the George W. Bush administration, she put together a team of Trump surrogates who gave daily briefings for Spanish-language media during the convention. This outreach effort continued for the presidential and vice-presidential debates and until the general election.

After the election victory, Aguirre Ferré and her team followed their boss, Sean Spicer, who went from RNC communications director to White House press secretary. But the incoming White House press team left the Office of Hispanic Media vacant, appointing Aguirre Ferré as director of media affairs instead. In a controversial move, the communications team also shut down the Spanish-language section of the White House website. The Twitter handle @LaCasaBlanca remained active, but not with daily postings.

Despite Aguirre Ferré's regular availability for interviews from the early days of the Trump administration until her departure in August 2018, the decision not to appoint a specific official for Hispanic media was a drastic departure from what had been interpreted as greater recognition by past administrations of the relevance of Spanish-language media.

To better understand the deep disappointment felt by the Spanish-language press corps that covers the White House and government agencies, go back to the early 1990s. It was the Clinton administration that realized that giving more access to Spanish-language media was the best way to reach the growing Latino community. Colleagues who covered that administration recall they were given constant access to many members of the Cabinet, which included three Hispanic secretaries and a Small Business administrator. Two Latinas, a White House deputy chief of staff, and an assistant press secretary were made available as well. For the first time, an administration placed many officials fluent in Spanish as spokespeople at key agencies, such as the State Department and the now-defunct Immigration and Naturalization Service.

The George W. Bush administration continued this trend, preserving the role of Hispanic spokespersons at the specialty-media press office at the White House. That office was led by four Hispanic directors, who performed the duties of Spanish-language spokespeople during the entire Bush administration. As in the previous administration, there was constant access to Cabinet members, which included three Hispanics, an SBA administrator, and two Latina treasurers of the United States.

During times of crisis such as the aftermath of the 9/11 attacks, or major administration initiatives such as immigration reform, there was even more access to Cabinet members and high-ranking officials. More importantly, there was access to the highest office, as President Bush sat for interviews with our network. The First Lady conducted sit-down interviews as well.

On a personal note, March 3, 2003, was my first day in my role as a Univision Washington correspondent, which happened to be the first day of the new Department of Homeland Security, created as a result of 9/11. The Bush administration placed fluent Spanish speakers as press officers at every one of the immigration-related agencies: the US Citizenship and Immigration Services, Immigration and Customs Enforcement, and Customs and Border Protection. Through the next six years of the Bush administration, we were granted unequaled access to the highest officials of those three agencies.

During the transition in late 2008, the incoming Obama administration decided it would put an even greater emphasis on Spanish-language press outreach, naming a director of a new White House Hispanic-media office. As in the past, the office reported to the main White House communications and press offices, which ultimately decided on whom and what they would make available in Spanish.

Barack Obama also granted us several one-on-one interviews and even took part in exclusive town halls aired by Univision and Telemundo. He also sat for interviews with anchors and reporters from local stations. Univision's New York and Los Angeles stations were among those invited to the White House for those interviews.

Following a tradition started by President Nixon and continued by President Reagan and both Bush administrations, Obama named a Latina as US treasurer. She stayed in office during his eight years as president. He named another Latina as SBA administrator, and four prominent Hispanics joined his Cabinet. All were constantly made available to Spanish-language media.

During Obama's first term, the unparalleled access to Labor Secretary Hilda Solis stood out. As a member of the Congressional Hispanic Caucus, she had been covered by many of us while she was in the House of Representatives. Shockingly, Obama named her to the Labor post, in spite of her having been a close adviser to Hillary Clinton's presidential campaign. At a time when millions of Americans were losing their jobs as a result of the 2008 financial crisis, for nearly two years she granted interviews to networks—Spanish and English—on the day the monthly unemployment report was released.

That said, not everything was rosy. During the past three administrations, Spanish-language reporters rarely were called on to ask questions during White House press briefings. Admittedly, for various reasons, our own presence in the briefing room was inconsistent.

Our constant and pressing need for Spanish-language interviews made it easy for all three administrations to better control their messages to the Latino community. The Obama administration took this a step further, sometimes allowing interviews only on topics that had been agreed on, unlike the then-regular White House press briefings, where reporters could ask questions freely.

On one hand, the Trump administration showed less interest in Spanish-language media than its predecessors. On the other, it would be unfair to say that we were completely shut out. Even if Univision was not granted sit-down interviews with President Trump or Vice President Mike Pence, our direct competitor, Telemundo, has been given those chances.

As immigration has figured so prominently as an administration priority since the campaign, it is no surprise that our coverage has focused on the Department of Homeland Security much more than before. Even if it did not match the high level of access during the George W. Bush administration, DHS and its agencies made officials available to Hispanic media, despite high personnel turnover.

The only Hispanic in Trump's Cabinet until his resignation in 2019, Labor Secretary Alex Acosta, was not made available for many interviews. However, the Trump administration offered interviews with the new SBA administrator, Jovita Carranza. The renegotiations of the trade accord with Mexico and Canada, another Trump priority, generated offers of coverage for Spanish-language media.

At the White House, there were no roundtables by the president with Hispanic media, as there were in the Obama administration. But other officials took on the role of Hispanic spokespeople. Mercedes Schlapp, who was director of specialty media during the George W. Bush administration, was appointed director of strategic communications in mid-2017 and was a Spanish-language spokeswoman until her departure in 2019. Carlos Diaz-Rosillo, deputy assistant to Trump and director of policy and interagency coordination until 2018, also was frequently an administration spokesperson on our broadcasts and online.

Many other federal agencies, however, lacked the Spanish-speaking press officers who were more common in the previous three administrations. Spanish-language outlets faced challenges with the Trump administration that were similar to those of English-language media. Our constant thirst for interviews in Spanish represented an extra obstacle for us with an administration that seemed uninterested or did not make communicating in Spanish a priority.

FERNANDO PIZARRO is supervising editor of NPR's *Morning Edition*. He has worked for CNN en Español, Associated Press Television, National Television of Chile, ESPN, NBC Canal de Noticias, Telefutura, and the Pan American Sports Network. He is an adjunct professor at American University.

THREE WEEKS

SERAFIN DANIEL "FIN" GOMEZ

I HAVE BEEN DELAYED in finishing this piece about covering President Trump because of the constraints of my day job—which is, of course, covering the White House.

A journalist assigned to cover the Trump White House had to move at a frenetic pace that, at times, rivaled riding a Coney Island roller coaster in a Category 4 hurricane as lightning bolts crash down and you suddenly realize that the car you are riding in has no safety harness. But three weeks of February and March 2020 came at an even more furious acceleration—even before the coronavirus.

"I am so exhausted," a White House press corps colleague confided while we waited for the president's last-minute Oval Office address to the nation on the coronavirus pandemic. It is a common phrase heard on the beat.

At seventy years old, President Trump was the oldest candidate to assume the presidency, but he has nearly the stamina of arguably our country's most energetic president, Theodore Roosevelt. While Teddy was an avid outdoorsman and fitness enthusiast, Trump has an indefatigable passion for tweeting at all hours, for watching television news—and, of course, for golf outings on the weekends. His White House staff members—many of whom are decades younger—have confirmed to me that he sleeps about four to five hours a night, starting his day at about 5:30 a.m. His staff has described him to me as a "nonstop ball of energy."

But some weeks accelerated to breakneck speed. I covered President Trump's Senate impeachment trial and his western-state swing as his re-election campaign revved up. Then, almost immediately, we traveled 8,114 miles to New Delhi for his state visit to the world's largest democracy.

At the invitation of Indian Prime Minister Narenda Modi, Trump and the First Lady went to Modi's home state of Gujarat, where he was the governor before he became head of state. His nationalist, populist streak parallels President Trump's own rise.

"The first lady and I have just traveled 8,000 miles around the world to deliver a message to every citizen across this nation. America loves India. America respects India—and America will always be faithful and loyal friends to the Indian people," Trump said to loud cheers at a rally with more than 100,000 Indian citizens in the world's largest (and on that day, seemingly the hottest) cricket stadium.

It was not an easy trip to arrange. Even though it was just an hour-long Air India flight to Gujarat, we had to deal with hauling large pieces of TV equipment—"the gear"—that we lug across the world to make sure we get our video and audio back to our viewers. We encountered long lines at airports, heightened security and at times a language barrier, even though English is the second language of India.

Our team of five landed in New Delhi just the day before we left for Ahmedabad to cover the largest Trump rally ever—even though the majority of the people in attendance were there more for Modi. The streets in Ahmedabad were lined with hundreds of large, festive posters about the historic visit. We raced through the city, swerving around the racing *tuk tuks* (motorized rickshaws) and revered cows waddling through busy intersections of this city of 700,000. This was so much different from the areas in the United States where Trump rallies have been held—and I have been to many. None was like this one.

It was hot, very hot, about 90 degrees during speeches by the two presidents. The stadium had no cover for us on the media riser, set in the middle of the blazing cricket field.

Despite the heat, the lack of sleep because of the time difference (and the fact that a producer from a Chinese network unexpectedly walked into my hotel room in the middle of the night because the hotel had double-booked us), the stress of broadcasting live from 7,000 miles away, using streaming technology that regularly works unless you are in a crowd of 100,000 using their cellphones, it was a phenomenal event to witness.

I was overcome with a sense of immense gratitude to be in that cricket stadium as an independent journalist and political junkie to observe 100,000 people cheering for issues that they believed would improve their part of the world.

"President Trump often judges events based on their size," my colleague Weijia Jiang, a CBS White House correspondent, reported during her live spot on CBS *This Morning:* "The bigger the better. So it is fitting that this stadium was absolutely packed with more than 100,000 people. The rally kicked off a whirlwind trip packed with the pageantry the president so loves. As both world leaders were surrounded by color, traditional music and dancing, the entire city of Ahmedabad has been transformed in a shrine to President Trump."

Before we left for our twenty-five-hour trip to New Delhi from Washington with a layover in Paris, Weijia and I had a deep conversation at the airport gate. Both of us were so excited to be part of the CBS team heading to India. Weijia also is one of the best moms I have known. She and I share parallels in our family backgrounds. We both have parents who were immigrants to the United States. My mother, who has died, came from El Salvador to the United States when she was eighteen to go to school in Washington, DC. Weijia's parents immigrated to the country from China and established their family and a successful restaurant in West Virginia.

"I keep thinking just how far we've come," I said to Weijia. "I am just so grateful."

On my first day, when I walked onto the White House grounds as an official White House producer, I teared up because it was the realization of a dream come true—a dream that started with *mi familia,* and everything they did to help me get here. My father worked his way through law school as a bag boy at a grocery store. My mother came here to study when she was eighteen with a belief that her children could amount to something. My grandfather, an airport janitor and later the owner of a small restaurant, never took a vacation, so he was able to raise twelve kids and put them through Catholic school. I thought about them all when I walked through the gates as a member of the White House press corps.

With that same inspiration and with encouragement from my colleagues at the White House and the National Association of Hispanic

Journalists, I decided to run for a seat on the board of the White House Correspondents' Association, one of the most important journalism organizations. My NAHJ friends pushed me in part because, in the 105-year history of the association, a Latino never had served on the board. Never.

Representation is so important in the broadcast-news industry. Whether it be on air, behind the camera, in the newsroom, or in the White House Briefing Room, representation matters.

Just after the July 4 holiday in 2019, the association announced that I had won the TV seat. Colleagues, including Weijia, who helped me write my campaign statement, congratulated me. But no congratulations mattered more than the one I got from a flip phone in Spain.

"I am proud of you," my father said from his home in Madrid. "I am proud of you."

"FIN" GOMEZ is a White House producer for CBS News. He has covered three presidential campaigns. He is the first Latino board member of the White House Correspondents' Association.

V

HE DISSEMBLES, BUT HE'S AVAILABLE— AND HIS THREATS DON'T COME TRUE

MAJOR GARRETT of CBS News wonders which is better—a president who "dissembles" or a president who is accessible. We had both in President Trump, he says. Paul Farhi of the *Washington Post* writes that the president's threats against the media are frightening—but that he doesn't follow through.

A FIREHOSE IN THE DESERT

MAJOR GARRETT

THE FUNDAMENTAL QUESTION in covering President Trump, the question around which every other journalistic inquiry about Trump coverage turns, is: Which type of president is better, an accessible dissembler or an aloof fact-teller?

Because clarity matters in this discussion, note that I said dissembler, not liar. Many have accused the president of lying and lying with a seemingly belligerent glee. I leave it to the voters to decide what is or is not a political or factual lie. That Trump dissembles is incontestable. He intentionally stretches or mangles facts for political, comedic, and dramatic effect. In my experience, no question I have asked congressional Republicans who support Trump has elicited more pauses and provoked more stammers than this: "What is President Trump's relationship to the truth?"

And, yet, Trump has been by far the most accessible president I have covered. He took questions relentlessly, sometimes twice or three times a day. He was more accessible by several orders of magnitude than Bill Clinton, George W. Bush, or Barack Obama. With Trump, impromptu press conferences in the Rose Garden, the Cabinet Room, or on the South Lawn were frequent and at times exceeded an hour. Trump allowed reporters to witness never-before-seen and unrehearsed policy conversations over immigration and gun control. He tweeted with abandon and appeared before cameras, often with little or no notice, to sometimes dizzying and precedent-defying effect.

On December 16, 2018, Trump held an extraordinary debate in the Oval Office with House Minority Leader Nancy Pelosi (soon to become House Speaker for a second time) and Senate Minority Leader Chuck Schumer. I stood in the Oval Office behind a couch, just inches away from Schumer's back and immediately to Trump's left. What was supposed to be a quick photo opportunity with the Democratic leaders—a nod to the new House Democratic majority-to-be—swiftly became a freewheeling tangle over a potential government shutdown, congressional funding for Trump's border wall, and who would suffer the political hit if a shutdown occurred.

After lengthy sparring over vote counts and Trump's legislative options, Pelosi said: "We're here to have a conversation in a prayerful way, so I don't think we should have a debate in front of the press on this." Trump kept hammering at legislative roadblocks in the Senate. Again, Pelosi said, "Let us have our conversation and meet with the press again." In both instances, Pelosi was looking at the White House press pool, of which I was a member, and bidding us to leave—even though she had no power to dismiss us. Trump had that power. The wrangling continued. Schumer jumped in, accusing Trump of misstating key facts about wall construction and trying to bully the Senate. Schumer and Trump spoke over one another, jousting in each other's direction, leaning in to press their points, raising their voices. I never had witnessed anything like this. For a third time, Pelosi sought a break in the action. "Let's call a halt to this." Schumer then joined the cause: "Let's debate in private."

Trump then called on me for a question. I asked if his definition of border security demanded new wall construction. I followed up to ask if that definition meant he was redefining "border security." This provoked more sparring between Trump, Schumer, and Pelosi, with all three addressing me during their respective answers. Again, this was without precedent in my coverage of four presidents. "Unfortunately, this has spiraled downward," Pelosi said. "This is a most unfortunate thing. We are entering into this kind of discussion in public view." Trump interjected: "But it's not bad, Nancy. It's called transparency." Pelosi's rejoinder cut to the heart of the Trump effect on news coverage of his presidency: "It's not transparency when we are not stipulating to a set of facts. We have to have an evidence-based conversation."

This is the conundrum of Trump coverage. On the one hand, Trump turned the Oval Office into a roiling stage where the two most powerful Democrats in Congress went toe-to-toe (nearly touching toes in the small confines) with Trump over immigration, wall construction, funding levels, and whether the government would or would not shut down. It was a genuine fight over priorities, policy, and politics. Reporters like me kept egging all sides on, just as we are supposed to do. It was crackling political theater. Trump trafficked in wild claims about terrorists caught at the border, undocumented immigrants bringing communicable diseases into the country, and an onslaught of illegal drugs "pouring into" America. Pelosi tried to bat those away. It played out on television in all its jarring, unscripted, and chirpy authenticity.

"You want to know something?" Trump said to Schumer in response to an allegation that his hard-line position would lead to a shutdown. "You want to put that on me. I'll take it. You know what I will say? Yes. If we don't get what we want one way or the other. I will shut down the government. I will take the mantle. I'm not going to blame you for it." That declaration weakened Trump's position in the new Congress. It led to the longest government shutdown in history without any legislative progress for Trump on border-wall funding, prompting him to declare a national emergency and siphon unspent Pentagon funds (something he hinted at during the clash with Pelosi and Schumer). Packed into that encounter one could find authentic political drama, honest argumentation, and a conclusion that carried lasting political consequences. All in full public view.

This is but one example of how available Trump makes himself to White House reporters. In my experience, it was the most vivid example of Trump's desire to make himself the central character in the daily drama that was *his* White House. It also displayed more memorably than any other event how Trump had a TV producer's eye and ear for conflict, intensity, and originality. Transparency is a plot device, one that makes for compelling TV and kept Trump at the center of every Washington story. Drama is its own political device, and Trump wielded it with unflinching confidence.

That's the firehose. The desert is what became of White House communication outside of Trump's own one-man show. Daily press briefings disappeared for a long period. Under Trump's first press secretary, Sean Spicer, they were psychodramas where Spicer came to the podium principally to prove himself to Trump—not answer questions. It began ingloriously with Spicer's very first briefing and the comic declaration, photographic evidence notwithstanding, that "this was the largest audience to ever witness an inauguration. Period."

The next press secretary, Sarah Sanders, typically kept her briefings to under twenty-five minutes unless a Cabinet official accompanied her (this was somewhat frequent during the Sanders era and is to be applauded). Near the end of her tenure, briefings all but disappeared. Trump announced Sanders's departure on June 13, 2019. Her last briefing had been March 11. It lasted fourteen minutes. There were no solo press-secretary briefings under Sanders's successor, Stephanie Grisham, as this is being written in spring 2020.

During the pandemic Trump led briefings on coronavirus response and became enamored of being a president "at war" and the comparatively high ratings that arose among information-starved households on lockdown. That metric obscured how the briefings—which sometimes ran longer than two hours and routinely lacked direction or coherence—over time cost Trump political support. They also laid the skeptical foundation for reopen-quick/masks-not-required sentiments in states led by Trump-aligned governors who, having followed this political tune, suffered devastating consequences in the summer of 2020 as the virus raged. Trump left it to Kayleigh McEnany, his fourth press secretary, to take up the brusque, content-free banner of Sanders's briefings. When the news turned savagely bad, Trump came back to the podium to revive the virus briefings. By then, he was being judged on his performance and suffering because the pandemic—unlike political rivals, the media, or twenty-first-century attention spans in general—cannot be insulted, distracted, or bullied into oblivion.

In general, if you ask me who do I want to hear from each day, the president or the press secretary, I always would say the president. The president shapes and decides policy. The president's voice is preeminent. Even so, the death of the daily briefing harms the press and the presidency. Every White House I covered before Trump (starting with Clinton and running through Bush and Obama) used the briefing to speak to the country and speak to itself. The briefing, on some occasions, created an internal pressure cooker on policy and public communication. Press secretaries for pre-Trump administrations shared with me and other reporters this observation about the power of daily briefings: that hard issues always were debated and sometimes resolved because of the anticipated pressure of briefing questions.

Throughout his presidency, when Trump held an impromptu press conference, the questions tended to hew to the center of the "news-of-the-day" lane. Plus, the atmosphere always was frenzied. On the South Lawn, reporters stuffed themselves together in a suffocating tight formation to catch Trump's eye. Reporters brayed at the top of their lungs. Questions had to be lightning quick. Coherent follow-ups were rare. This also was true when only the White House press pool puts questions to Trump—it's always that day's news; the quarters are cramped and the opportunity to dig in on an issue is extremely limited. Historically, daily briefings allowed for more follow-ups, nuance, and variety.

That does not mean White House briefings were perfect. They could be tedious. They could suffer from Beltway groupthink. They could become stages for contrived friction. The public could and often did see through those flaws.

What remained, however, was a permanent and searchable record of an administration's orientation to policy, legislation, or an unexpected crisis. The briefings became a kind of daily diary that reporters, historians, and the public could revisit. Without briefings (and often *with* them), the country could see nothing of the Trump White House but Trump; the grand impresario, the TV producer, the perpetual voice box of his turbulent reign.

Which brings me to "enemy of the people." No president ever has spoken like this about a free and independent press. For Trump, it was part truth and part trope. At one level, he believed reporters were out to get him (as have previous presidents). At another level, he delighted in turning the fate of the press and its credibility and market share (both in decline since the mid-1990s) into a commercial and rhetorical cudgel.

Trump beat on the press because he knew that the press was so down. Networks are not as powerful as they once were. Dominant newspapers are less able to shape public opinion. Weekly news magazines have disappeared or atrophied to gaunt wispiness. In a world of atomized journalism and opinion, a dominant voice retains more power. All my interactions with Trump tell me that is his aim—to project power by being the unignorable sound, the voice that, welcome or not, permeates every crevice of American consciousness.

But this is more than a device or a tactic. Under Trump, it was changing behavior and inspiring crass imitation. This is a future danger Trump alone has unleashed. On January 28, 2020, Trump announced in the East Room his plan for Middle East peace. He paused during those remarks to thank Secretary of State Mike Pompeo. Sitting right behind Pompeo was Alan Dershowitz, a significant legal scholar and civil libertarian. "Our great secretary of state, Mike Pompeo," Trump said. Applause filled the room. "Whoa. Oh, that's impressive. That was very impressive, Mike." Laughter ensued. Trump continued: "That reporter couldn't have done too good a job on you yesterday, right?" More laughter. At that moment, Dershowitz, also laughing, tapped Pompeo affectionately on the back. Trump continued: "I think you did a good job on her actually. That's good. Thank you, Mike. Great."

Trump was referring to a clash Pompeo had the week before with Mary Louise Kelly of National Public Radio's *All Things Considered.* Pompeo objected to Kelly's questions on Ukraine policy and whether he had publicly defended Marie Yovanovitch, the ousted US ambassador to Ukraine. Pompeo tried to deflect the questions by arguing they were off limits. Kelly reminded Pompeo that his staff knew Ukraine questions would be asked. Eventually, a State Department staffer abruptly ended the interview, as NPR listeners heard when it was played in full.

According to Kelly, Pompeo then summoned her into another room and berated her with obscenities. "I was taken to the secretary's private living room where he was waiting and where he shouted at me for about the same amount of time as the interview itself," Kelly said. "He asked, 'Do you think Americans care about Ukraine?' He used the F-word in that sentence and many others." Pompeo did not dispute Kelly's account of their post-interview interaction. He accused her, however, of violating "the basic rules of journalism and decency."

Days later, the State Department dropped a different NPR reporter from traveling aboard Pompeo's plane for a trip to Europe and Central Asia. Pompeo's attempt to limit Kelly's interview, his abusive treatment of

Kelly afterward, and the State Department's decision to eliminate NPR's already approved presence on Pompeo's next trip all signify a bristling hostility to and intolerance of a free, unintimidated, and probing press corps. Trump's subsequent lavish praise of Pompeo is one thing. Dershowitz's utterly natural acceptance and tactile gesture of support for Pompeo personified a kind of startling transference. Trump's anti-press hostility had, in this moment, become ceremonially normalized.

So much about Trump was neither normal nor previously observed. The consequences were as varied as they were unknowable. Trump was accessible. Trump was a TV producer. Trump dissembled. Trump was the president of a reality show that was by turns real and unreal. It amused, bemused, and horrified. The only constant was Trump's fervent willingness—his overwhelming need—to be the ever-watched ringmaster of all three.

Trump commands attention and spins news cycles with a mixture of improvisation, impetuosity, and conflict-driven purpose. He is unlike any political figure I have covered. Journalists, scholars, political scientists, and historians will study his methods and their consequences for decades; in this, Trump will be the subject of perpetual debate and fascination—a firehose in the desert.

MAJOR GARRETT is the chief Washington correspondent for CBS News. Previously, he was the network's chief White House correspondent. He is the author or coauthor of four books, including *Mr. Trump's Wild Ride: The Thrills, Chills, Screams, and Occasional Blackouts of an Extraordinary Presidency.*

HIS BARK IS WORSE
THAN HIS BITE

PAUL FARHI

EVER SINCE HE RODE Trump Tower's golden escalator down to a press conference to announce his candidacy in 2015, President Trump made his contempt for the mainstream news media an integral part of his "brand." Denouncing reporters was a surefire crowd-pleaser at his campaign rallies, a near-daily obsession of his Twitter feed, an article of faith among the Trump faithful. In TrumpWorld, it almost was a cleansing ritual: the press must be regularly denigrated and delegitimized.

So, what did Trump actually accomplish by being the news media's daily scourge? The answer is both a lot and very little. Trump's diatribes didn't cause the press to go easier on him; if anything, the daily coverage of the president is just as tough and rigorous as it always has been. Nor have his fulminations led to any practical limitations on press freedom. Nevertheless, I'd argue that Trump's beat-the-press rhetoric reaped a huge return on investment—for Trump, if no one else.

Let's start on November 7, 2018. I was driving home from work that night when I glanced down at a text message that had flashed on my phone. "Acosta out," it read. "WH suspended. Need you back." The message from an editor was easy enough to decipher: The White House had just suspended CNN reporter Jim Acosta, who earlier that day had engaged in a tense back-and-forth with President Trump at a press conference. Trump had reacted with visible irritation as Acosta fired questions at him and a White House intern tried to take his microphone away. Acosta was an annoyance, a preexisting condition for Trump and the White House press staff, which seethed about his "grandstanding."

As I headed back to the office to write the story, the news seemed ominous, at least to someone like me, a reporter who writes about other reporters. The president was taking an unprecedented step—banning a journalist who'd gotten under his skin from entering the White House grounds. Could he do that? Was that even legal?

As it turned out, the answer was no, he couldn't. CNN sued a few days after Trump banned Acosta. A federal judge (a Trump appointee, no less) agreed with CNN that Trump's action violated the Constitution, specifically, the Fifth Amendment guarantee of due process (he didn't rule on whether it violated the First Amendment's guarantee of press freedom). He ordered the White House to restore Acosta's access, and Acosta was quickly back at work.

In hindsight, the Acosta episode seems like a metaphor for Trump's behavior toward the press. It's full of dramatic statements, lots of color, and even some action. But his statements—shocking at first glance, questionable on second thought—amounted to little. It's part of a pattern: Trump talked a good (or perhaps very bad) game against the press, but in practical terms it's only meaningful as another set piece staged to please Trump's supporters.

Trump used the Acosta Model time and again. And, time and again, his actions and threats essentially have come to nothing:

- Remember the reports immediately after the election that Trump was considering moving the White House press out of the White House press room, effectively exiling journalists from the grounds? Sounded very tough. It didn't happen.

- Remember Trump's campaign-trail musings about "opening up" libel laws to make it easier to sue news organizations for reporting things he didn't like? Also didn't happen.

- Remember Trump's many threats to sue news organizations for libel, after one or more stories about his taxes, his charity scam, or his alleged assaults on women? Trump (or at least his campaign) *has* sued media outlets, but not over those things.

- Remember Trump's unusual practice of signing White House employees to nondisclosure agreements (NDAs), the better to muzzle them from speaking to the press (or writing books) after their service was complete? The NDAs did muzzle some employees . . . until they didn't. In a little-noticed settlement in November 2019, the president's lawyers dropped an effort to enforce the terms of an NDA against Cliff Sims, a former White House aide who wrote a tell-all book (*Team of Vipers*) about his brief stint in the president's employ. There always was some question about whether the NDAs were legally enforceable; the settlement with Sims was an effective admission that they weren't, or at least that Trump had no desire to invoke their terms if challenged.

Trump's efforts to torpedo the well-established traditions and norms regarding the press and the president largely failed because the courts and the Constitution won't let him succeed. Just as Acosta's dismissal was quickly overturned by a federal court, so was Trump's attempt last summer to impose a thirty-day ban on a second White House reporter, Brian Karem of *Playboy* magazine. After *Playboy* sued on Karem's behalf, a second federal judge saw his suspension the way the judge had in the Acosta case: as a violation of Karem's due-process rights. He, too, sent Karem right back to work. Trump hasn't tried to ban any reporters since then.

Trump's campaign sued the *New York Times, Washington Post,* and CNN in early March 2020 for defamation over opinion articles that linked the campaign to Russian election meddling in 2016. Legal experts called the suits frivolous, effectively a publicity stunt to amplify Trump's criticisms of the news media. The reason: Public officials, let alone presidents, must prove that a publisher acted with "reckless disregard" for the truth, that is, knew a published statement was false but published it anyway—an almost impossible bar for the campaign to clear. What's more, op-ed columns, by definition, are opinions, which courts have held cannot be declared defamatory.

Similarly, Trump can't "open up" libel laws because those are beyond the reach of the president. Libel is a state matter. Whatever federal libel standards there are reside in the Constitution's First Amendment and in the Supreme Court's interpretation of it. Trump's juggernaut of federal judicial appointments may lead to a reinterpretation of state libel laws, but the president can't take any direct action to make this happen.

For all his blunt talk, Trump took only one action that has materially hurt the news media. He never formally declared an end to the long tradition of White House briefings, but end they did, on March 11, 2019. The Trump White House went more than a year without holding a daily briefing. Instead of giving briefings that were open and available to all (including the public), his press secretary effectively privatized her job by speaking nearly exclusively to Fox News, a reliably friendly outlet. She also played press critic on Twitter, regularly hammering reporting and commentary unfavorable to her boss.

The reason Trump cancelled the briefings—beyond his fury over seeing his spokespeople confronted daily by reporters like Acosta—is because he could. It was the one, perhaps the only, action he could take that no court or second party could gainsay. It projected his dominance over the fake-news purveyors (never mind that the White House press corps also includes journalists whose TV networks and publications generally or even reflexively support Trump). All the better that media figures regularly protest and complain about the briefing's demise; that some members of the press don't like it is justification for it in the first place. (Trump himself doesn't give many formal press conferences, preferring to take questions during Oval Office "sprays" and before helicopter departures from the South Lawn of the White House, both venues in which journalists are barely heard and little seen.)

And that's the key to understanding Trump's press-baiting, press-hating strategy. It's a shadow game, with the press used as props. His real audience is at home, watching and cheering as the populist president takes on the hated Establishment, in this case something called "the media."

With the dawn of the coronavirus pandemic, Trump found that he needed the press after all. Not only were the daily briefings revived under a new press secretary, Kayleigh McEnany, but Trump appeared near daily at first in the press room for updates about the government's response to the crisis. It was, of course, easy to understand Trump's renewed desire to speak to reporters in these televised sessions: The country faced an enormous health and economic crisis, and Trump's poll numbers were plummeting amid them. Trump pegged much of his reelection chances to his ability to persuade Americans he was on top of things.

Trump has long played into the widely held distrust of the people and organizations who cover him. But this distrust predates Trump by many decades; he's just gotten in front of the parade. Overall, the percentage of Americans who told Gallup they have a "great deal" or "fair amount" of trust in the media's ability to report accurately fell to just 32 percent during the 2016 campaign, the lowest figure in the forty-seven years Gallup has been asking the question.

But the upshot of Trump's constant war on the news media isn't that more people distrust the press. Perversely, it turns out that more people actually trust the news media than when Trump was elected. Despite Trump's constant badgering, or perhaps as a rejection of it, Gallup has recorded an uptick in media trust over the past three years. In 2019, some 41 percent were in the great deal/fair amount column.

The more important question, however, is who isn't in that column. As it happens, the slight increases in trust were driven almost entirely by self-identified Democrats and independents. Among Republicans— Trump's base—the "trust" measure virtually has collapsed since 2015, not coincidentally the year Trump came down that golden escalator.

In other words, despite his constant bullying from the bully pulpit, Trump didn't appreciably change public opinion about the press. He's only changed it among his supporters, which may have been his goal all along. I guess that's "winning."

Which brings me back to Jim Acosta's suspension. The day his White House press pass was reinstated, Acosta went back to work. Little more was heard of the episode. Trump hasn't sought to isolate him or undermine him further; he's even taken questions from him during Oval Office pool "sprays."

To a superficial observer, the right of access had been preserved and the free press had been validated. But, to his supporters, Trump had triumphed again. He'd fought another battle, delivered the right message. Mission: accomplished.

PAUL FARHI covers the news media for the *Washington Post*.

VI

IT'S BEEN BAD BEFORE, BUT NOT THIS BAD

STEVE THOMMA WRITES about other presidents who haven't liked the media. (That's almost all of them.) He looks back from a unique position: Steve is executive director of the White House Correspondents' Association. Clark Hoyt, recalling that he covered the Nixon resignation, says that the system almost always has worked in the past. Will it now? Alexis Simendinger of *The Hill* says that everyone wonders, "Can we go back to the way it used to be?" Quint Forgey, a young reporter with *Politico*, has a slightly different take: "Has it always been this way?"

TRUMP'S PREDECESSORS WOULD ENVY HIS USE OF TWITTER

STEVE THOMMA

FROM THE DAY HE TOOK OFFICE, President Donald Trump found what his predecessors had sought for nearly a century—a way to communicate their message to the American people *in their own fashion,* over the heads of the White House press corps and unfiltered by the news media that disseminated their stories to the world.

Franklin D. Roosevelt tried it with his Fireside Chats on radio. John F. Kennedy did, too, with nationally televised addresses to the nation. Ronald Reagan added the Hollywood element, aides staging the background images of presidential events so that they would convey thematic messages regardless of what the media voices were saying.

Barack Obama ushered in a whole new era, using the tools of the Internet to send self-selected and produced images and video straight to the country while often shutting out the photojournalists of the White House press altogether.

Then came Trump, using Twitter to blast his thoughts straight at tens of millions of followers. The ease of social media allowed him not only to speak to millions unfiltered by the news media but to both undermine the press and drive their daily news agenda all at the same time.

"Donald Trump's brash, often reckless, use of Twitter has enabled him to communicate directly to the public, stage-manage his political allies and detractors, and control the news agenda," wrote Diana Owen, a political-science professor at Georgetown University, in her report, "The Past Decade and Future of Political Media: The Ascendance of Social Media." "Aided by social media," she said of Trump, "he has exceeded the ability of his modern-day presidential predecessors to achieve these ends."

The press still was there, in the Trump White House, in the president's motorcade, on Air Force One. Challenged, to be sure. Scathing rhetoric about the media. The shutdown for more than a year of daily briefings that allowed reporters to ask detailed follow-up questions. Americans, while they increasingly get their news from Twitter and other social media, still look to the traditional media—and thus the White House press—for news about the president, at least for now. And President Trump still took questions from the press corps to ensure he is in their coverage. At times, the driveway outside the White House briefing room was a traffic jam of ladders that photojournalists need to get images of the president when he holds court on his way to the helicopter on the South Lawn.

But, even before they get to the White House each morning, reporters looked at Twitter to learn what President Trump was saying. Predecessors would have marveled at the communications tools of the twenty-first-century president.

Take FDR, who invented the twentieth-century model of presidential communication. He didn't trust the news media to get his message out the way he intended. Fears of bias against the president drove the White House even then. What to do? Go straight to the people. He did exactly that just a week into his presidency, going on the radio in the first of his Fireside Chats to talk to the country without any filter of news stories in the daily newspapers. "He and his advisers worried that newspapers' biases would affect the news columns and rightly so," said Betty Houchin Winfield in her book on FDR's communications skills. Radio offered the president a different path. "It cannot misrepresent or misquote," said Press Secretary Stephen Early.

A change, sure? But not as revolutionary as myth suggests. FDR still relied mainly on the press to get his message out. In his first term, he held a staggering 337 press conferences. Across twelve years, he talked directly to the people via Fireside Chats only thirty times—an average of less than three a year.

Take Kennedy. He turned to television, talking straight into the lens and American living rooms in national addresses, such as during the Cuban Missile Crisis. CBS News called him "our first television president." But he also talked to the press a lot, holding sixty-four full, formal news conferences in the roughly thirty-four months of his presidency.

As late as George W. Bush, that remained the model, with occasional efforts to talk directly to the people via radio or television with a full complement of coverage by the press corps through full presidential press conferences, interviews with the president, and daily briefings by the press secretary.

Obama became the father of twenty-first-century presidential communication, changing the game with his use of the Internet and social media as a pathway around the press. His White House started sending its own photos and videos directly to followers on social media, frequently from events where photojournalists were banned.

In June 2013, for example, the White House allowed a single news photo of Obama alone when he visited Nelson Mandela's former prison cell at Robben Island in South Africa. The White House banned news coverage of Obama's family joining him in the cell. It was, the White House said, a "private" moment.

Yet White House photographer Pete Souza snapped a photo of Obama hugging his daughter in the cell, an emotional moment which was released directly to the public. And White House videographers recorded the visit for a video released by the White House and narrated by Michelle Obama. "This is just like Tass," New York Times photographer Doug Mills told White House Press Secretary Jay Carney in a reference to the former Soviet Union government "news" agency.

There were more, including meetings with Hillary Clinton, the Congressional Hispanic Caucus, African American faith leaders, and Israeli and Palestinian negotiators. On October 11, 2013, Obama, again with family members, met with Palestinian human rights activist Malala Yousafzai. Again, the press was kept out. Again, the White House released its own photo of the purportedly "private" moment.

The issue came to a head in November 2013 when a coalition of news outlets and associations, including the White House Correspondents' Association, joined in protest. "The apparent reason for closing certain events to photographers is that these events have been deemed private.

That rationale, however, is undermined when the White House releases its own photograph of a so-called private event through social media," the journalists said in a letter to the White House. "You are in effect replacing independent photojournalism with visual press releases."

The White House insisted it was only using newly available social media as well as e-mail to better inform the American people. "We've taken advantage of new technology to give the American public even greater access to behind-the-scenes footage or photographs of the president doing his job," said then–Principal Deputy Press Secretary Josh Earnest. "I understand why that is a source of some consternation to the people in this room, but, to the American public, that is a clear win. That is people having access because of new technology to things that they've never seen before. . . . But that has never been viewed internally here at the White House as a substitute for the important work that's done by free and independent journalists."

Obama, though, did continue to take questions from the news media, in formal presidential news conferences and interviews, and his press secretary continued to hold daily news briefings.

For Trump, the new medium of choice was Twitter. It allowed him to say anything he desired without filter at any hour, regardless of whether the news media wanted to cover what he said.

He used it to communicate policy directly at home and abroad. In September 2017, for example, he used Twitter to talk directly to North Korea President Kim Jong-un, as well as all of Trump's Twitter followers at home. He called Kim "Rocket Man," reaching tens of millions of his followers and seizing the news agenda for days.

In June 2018, he used Twitter to slam French President Emmanuel Macron and Canadian Prime Minister Justin Trudeau over trade, setting off a Twitter spat that ended with Trump leaving a summit early.

In January 2019, he used it to notify Congress—and threaten Iran—of possible military action: "These Media Posts will serve as notification to the United States Congress that should Iran strike any U.S. person or target, the United States will quickly & fully strike back, & perhaps in a disproportionate manner."

He's used it to vent boasts and grievances. He tweeted frequently about a 95 percent approval rating from Republicans, though fact-checkers could find that in any publicly available poll. He tweets often as well that journalists are "fake news" and an "enemy of the people."

On one day alone in January 2020, as the Senate started its trial of Trump's impeachment, he tweeted or retweeted more than 140 times, a record, according to *Politico* and Factba.se, a site that tracks Trump's tweets. Between midnight and 1:00 a.m. alone, he tweeted 41 times, a rate of 1 every 88 seconds.

His communications via tweet were magnified in a country where social media are rising fast as a source for news, and the White House for a long period essentially shut down the daily news briefings that allowed reporters to ask for clarifications and details about what the president was saying. Some days, Trump's tweets are the only official news out of the White House.

"Donald Trump's brash, often reckless, use of Twitter has enabled him to communicate directly to the public, stage-manage his political allies and detractors, and control the news agenda," wrote Owen. "Aided by social media, he has exceeded the ability of his modern-day presidential predecessors to achieve these ends."

This came as the share of American adults getting news from social media "often" or "sometimes" jumped 10 points from 2016 to 2019, from 44 percent to 54 percent, according to the Pew Research Center.

"The president has tweeted or retweeted more than 300 times in the past five days," former press secretary Stephanie Grisham said on Fox News January 26, 2020, when asked why she ended daily news briefings. "So that is people, not just the media, but the American public hearing directly from him, every single day, several times a day." Rather than seeing her job as helping reporters get more information, she suggested she saw it as unhelpful. "There is no way . . . I could say anything better than what he's saying on his own. And, then again, he's always doing press conferences." That's likely because there still is an audience for the traditional news media covering the White House.

Television, new websites, and radio remained the top source of news as of 2018, according to Pew. The breakdown of where people "often" got news in 2018 versus 2016:

- TV: 49 percent, down from 57 percent
- news websites: 33 percent, up from 26 percent;
- radio: 26 percent, up from 25 percent
- social media: 20 percent, up from 18 percent;
- newspapers: 16 percent, down from 20 percent

Yet the numbers are shifting fast, and demographics suggest many more challenges ahead. When the national numbers are broken up by age group, it becomes clear that older Americans skew the audience toward traditional media. Youngest Americans skew greatly toward social media.

The breakdown of where people sixty-five and older "often" got news in 2018:

- TV: 81 percent
- newspapers: 39 percent
- radio: 30 percent
- news sites: 28 percent
- social media: 8 percent

Now look at the news sources for those aged eighteen to twenty-nine:

- social media: 36 percent
- news sites: 27 percent
- TV: 16 percent
- radio: 13 percent
- newspapers: 2 percent

So, as Trump built on a new era of presidents finding a way to talk to people over the heads of the White House press, younger Americans already are more open to new sources of news. That is a landscape with more challenges for the press.

STEVEN THOMMA covered the White House for Knight Ridder and Mc-Clatchy. He is now the executive director of the White House Correspondents' Association. He speaks here for himself and not for the WHCA.

DOES THE SYSTEM STILL WORK?

CLARK HOYT

ON THURSDAY, AUGUST 8, 1974, I was among the crowd of reporters packed into the White House press room, awaiting President Richard Nixon's announcement that he would resign in the face of certain impeachment by the House and removal by the Senate.

Suddenly, the door leading to the press secretary's suite of offices opened and a young aide I'd never seen before came striding out, angrily pushing his way through. There were loud slamming sounds. The aide disappeared, and we discovered we'd been locked in. We couldn't enter the offices. We couldn't exit to the outside. The tension, already high, rose. What next, someone joked darkly, poison gas through the air-conditioning vents?

Then, as mysteriously as they'd been locked, the doors were unlocked, and the wait for the president's speech continued. Only much later would we learn why we'd been briefly imprisoned. A distraught Nixon, at times sobbing uncontrollably, had been taking a final walk with his Irish setter, King Timahoe, around the grounds of the White House. The staff, many enraged at the assembled news media, whom they blamed in large part for their boss's downfall, did not want us to see and be able to report on him in such a state.

Conflict, hard feelings, even flashes of hatred have been built into the relationship between presidents and press since the founding of the Republic. Franklin Roosevelt, a master at shaping his message, once told a reporter for the *New York Times* to put on a dunce cap and stand in the corner for persisting in asking a question FDR didn't want to answer. Harry Truman complained more than sixty years ago that "presidents and the members of their Cabinets and their staff members have been slandered and misrepresented since George Washington." He described some journalists as "paid prostitutes of the mind." Barack Obama's administration initiated more prosecutions of leaks to reporters on national-security grounds than all his predecessors combined.

We're fond of quoting Thomas Jefferson's saying that he'd have chosen newspapers without a government over a government without newspapers. We'd just as soon forget how upset he became at the partisan press of his time, declaring, "Nothing can now be believed which is seen in a newspaper."

Jefferson and Truman did their complaining in private letters. Donald Trump tweeted his rage to 60 million followers. Prior presidents may have seethed over coverage of their administrations, but in public they at least paid lip service to the role of an independent media as an important check on unbridled government power. Not Trump, who declared that the press is "truly the enemy of the people."

To be sure, disaffection from the mainstream news media had been building, especially on the right, for decades. Nixon sent his vice president, Spiro Agnew, to rail against "nattering nabobs of negativism" who, he said, "have formed their own 4-H club—the hopeless, hysterical hypochondriacs of history." George W. Bush's chief of staff, Andrew Card, told Ken Auletta of the *New Yorker* that the media "don't represent the public any more than other people do. . . . I don't believe you have a check-and-balance function." Trump just went the final step. The president himself declared journalists who aren't members of his Fox News fan club to be part of an illegitimate opposition—not to be respected, not to be believed.

He was aided and abetted by forces within social media, the Internet, Fox and other right-wing outlets, which long have been undermining trust in media that operate with professional standards of fact-based reporting, fairness, and objectivity.

And, even before them, on the old medium of radio. Rush Limbaugh denounced what he called "the Four Corners of Deceit: Government, academia, science, and the media," which he claimed "live in the Universe of Lies."

So, when fact-checkers at the *Washington Post* report that Trump made more than twenty-thousand false or misleading statements in his first twenty-seven months in office—an astonishing total that surely would disqualify any other person from public trust and office—Trump's following is conditioned to dismiss it as just another baseless attack from the opposition.

The president's public hostility toward individual reporters was unprecedented. When Jim Acosta of CNN attempted at a news conference to ask Trump a question he didn't like, the president cut him off and called Acosta "a rude, terrible person." The White House then suspended Acosta's press credential, later backing down after CNN filed a federal lawsuit.

What starts at the top carries down through the administration. Trump's was the first White House in history to have a press secretary who never held a briefing for reporters, once a daily event. Stephanie Grisham, formerly the president's official spokeswoman, rarely gave interviews—and, when she did, it was to Fox, One America News Network, and the Sinclair Broadcast Group, all outlets on the right. Unlike her predecessors, Grisham clearly did not see her job as a bridge between the president and inquiring reporters. Instead, she was a pugnacious advocate, ready to go the boss one better with crude insults. Trump said Republicans who didn't support him were "human scum." Grisham declared that the term should be applied to anyone who criticized Trump.

In such an administration, it should be no surprise that probing questions were greeted with anger and scorn. When Mary Louise Kelly of National Public Radio asked Secretary of State Mike Pompeo about something he didn't want to address, his failure to publicly support the ousted ambassador to Ukraine, Pompeo summoned her into his private living room and launched into a profanity-laced tirade against her that Kelly said lasted about as long as their nine-minute broadcast interview. She said Pompeo then had an aide bring a map of the world with the names of countries omitted and challenged Kelly to find Ukraine on it. When she did, he ended their meeting.

The next day, the State Department issued a statement from Pompeo declaring that Kelly had lied to him twice, first by failing to honor a promise to restrict the interview to questions about Iran and then by failing to keep their subsequent conversation off the record. E-mails between Kelly and Pompeo's press aide showed it was the secretary who wasn't telling the truth in the first instance. The reporter had specifically refused to limit the subject matter to Iran. Two eyewitnesses from NPR said there was no agreement that the later conversation with Pompeo would be off the record, and Kelly said she never would have made one. Days later, in an apparent act of spite, another NPR reporter was barred from a Pompeo trip to Europe and Central Asia.

In today's hyper-partisan Washington, it is impossible to imagine a repeat of the circumstances that led to Nixon's decision to resign. The House Judiciary Committee in late July 1974 had voted to recommend impeachment of the president for obstructing the investigation of the break-in at Democratic national headquarters in the Watergate and covering up other unlawful activities, such as misuse of the Internal Revenue Service for political purposes. Six of the committee's seventeen Republicans joined all of the Democrats.

On August 5, after a unanimous Supreme Court ordered Nixon to turn over unredacted tape recordings of his Watergate-related conversations to Special Counsel Leon Jaworski, the "smoking gun" came into public view: Nixon had discussed with his chief of staff, H. R. Haldeman, a plan, based on false grounds that national security had been involved, to get the CIA to ask the FBI to stop investigating the break-in. Two days later, Senator Barry Goldwater and the Republican leaders of the Senate and House met with the president in the Oval Office and told him he had lost the support of his party and surely would be convicted.

In contrast, Trump was impeached on a party-line vote in the House. Only one Republican in the Senate, Mitt Romney of Utah, voted with Democrats to convict, after his party blocked any testimony from direct witnesses to the president's actions.

Would today's Supreme Court, increasingly a partisan battleground, have ruled unanimously as the high court did during Watergate that the president's White House tapes had to be released? Had there been Twitter, Fox, and InfoWars, what would have happened to a John Dean after he testified at the Senate Watergate hearings, or to Alexander Butterfield, arguably the man most responsible for Nixon's downfall? It was Butterfield, the former deputy chief of staff, who revealed the existence of the White House taping system, and one can only imagine the abuse and threats that would have showered down on him from Nixon loyalists in today's media world.

Look what happened to John Bolton, Trump's former national-security adviser, when it was revealed that he was prepared to provide damaging testimony at the president's Senate impeachment trial. Bolton, long a conservative hawk and contributor to Fox News, was overnight a pariah. The turnabout was so instant and ill thought out that it was sometimes laughable. Fox's Lou Dobbs called Bolton a "TOOL FOR THE LEFT" and said the evidence was that he used the same literary agency as James Comey, the FBI director fired by Trump. One of the agency's partners quickly pointed out in a tweet to Dobbs that Dobbs himself was also a client. "Are you part of the conspiracy?" he asked.

On Friday, August 9, 1974, I stood with other reporters on a hastily constructed riser on the South Lawn of the White House, waiting for the Nixon family to emerge after the president's emotional farewell address to his staff. About to be an ex-president at noon, Nixon climbed the steps of his waiting helicopter, turned and raised his arms in a bizarre victory pose, then was flown off into history.

Shortly afterward, I watched in the East Room as Chief Justice Warren Burger administered the oath of office to President Gerald Ford. In a brief address to the overflow crowd of more than three hundred and a national television audience, Ford said, "As we bind up the internal wounds of Watergate, more painful and more poisonous than those of foreign wars, let us restore the Golden Rule to our political process and let brotherly love purge our hearts of suspicion and hate." At the end of the ceremony, Burger, tears in his eyes, put his hand on the shoulder of Senate Minority Leader Hugh Scott, a Republican from Pennsylvania, and said, "Thank God, it works."

Once again our political system and society are under great stress. Time will tell whether it still will work.

CLARK HOYT formerly was Washington editor of Knight Ridder and public editor of the *New York Times*. He won the Pulitzer Prize for national reporting in 1973.

A PRESIDENT WHO UNIQUELY UNDERMINES CONFIDENCE IN THE MEDIA

ALEXIS SIMENDINGER

AS A REPORTER who has covered a handful of presidents and occasionally speaks to audiences about what's in the news, I've heard versions of one particular question over and over since 2017: "Do you think we can ever go back?"

Some people ask me whether the presidency—and they include White House communications—can "go back" to something they perceive as more conventional and trustworthy. Others ask if the news media can "go back" to reporting with more rigor and less of whatever they think is damaging or exhausting about what we're doing.

My answer is always "yes and no," with anecdotes.

I've heard forms of this question from women and men, young professionals and mid-career civil servants, liberals and conservatives, and Americans who are geographically dispersed. What they share is a sense of unease, either about how President Trump operated (and the ramifications), or how the news media report on national and political news out of Washington. Often both. It says something about our times that so many voters look backwards, sometimes wistfully, for reassurances about what's to come. Regardless of partisan sensibilities, they worry that Washington's guardrails have been blown off and won't be recovered.

Can the American presidency go back? Yes, sort of.

Let's play a mind game. If Trump somehow had decided to hand the presidency to Mike Pence, would Pence operate and communicate like Trump? Treat the news media and the institutions of government the same way? No.

Most of us can agree that Pence, a social conservative with a dozen years of congressional experience and a term as Indiana's governor before becoming Trump's number two, never has been drawn to phrases such as "*your favorite president, me!*"

Trump is a personality-driven enterprise. His "American carnage" worldview and particularly self-referential political antennae retire with him. My point is obvious: no one is like the forty-fifth president, and number forty-six is likely to be the un-Trump.

"PRESIDENTS COME AND GO. Some leave their mark, some fade into memory," former president Johnson said in 1965. My theory of the pendulum begins in 1992. Former president Bill Clinton, grasping for a little of JFK's aura, persuaded voters during a recession that he was the youthful, future-focused antidote to a Republican. Former president George W. Bush, with some help from the Supreme Court, persuaded voters in 2000 that he was an ethical "compassionate conservative" who would not burden Americans with political schemes and finger-to-wind decision-making.

"I did what I did and ultimately history will judge," Bush said somewhat defensively in 2013 at his presidential library in Texas.

Bush's war footing after two terms sparked a revival of grassroots hope and change, sending Democrat Barack Obama to the White House with voters' instructions to end global conflicts and dig the middle class out of a financial abyss with new jobs and some health coverage.

Trump followed Obama, turning his own presidency into a transparent rebuke of his predecessor and his policies. A survey in January 2020 found some startling appraisals of Trump: Majorities of Americans said they believe Trump acted illegally and unethically, according to the Pew Research Center's American Trends Panel. The poll results were a clue about changes before the pandemic and recession.

That's not to suggest Trump's record will fade away. The country has a more conservative Supreme Court, expanded executive power, and partisan mistrust in hallmarks of government and democracy. After his 2016 victory, Trump told Americans, and even visiting heads of state, that the press is "corrupt," "the enemy of the people" and "fake news."

Every president I've covered has been unhappy with the news media at times, impatient with the White House press corps, and yearned to exploit communications technology to work around the press "filter." But, in my experience, Trump stirred unique enthusiasm for undermining trust in the news media when his predecessors avoided such combat or were convinced it would undermine their goals.

But much has changed. Americans get their news and information everywhere, even as local newspaper and community coverage dies. Americans self-select news sources. By and large, the public wants information that's free, fast, and entertaining. Google and Facebook are now the editors. Disinformation and manipulated content travel within seconds on the Internet. And just 22 percent of the US public uses Twitter—and only a tiny percentage of users is responsible for the majority of tweets about politics. The loud minority lend their voices to Twitter, amplified by major media outlets that cover them.

Can the news media "go back"? No. When I'm asked that question, it's often by someone who believes the news media at large are liberal, biased, error-prone, and elitist. The questioners want to know if the media can undertake some course corrections. In their minds, the news business of the past was superior. Frustrated, they ask for suggestions. "*What should I read to get the truth?*"

I am sympathetic. News outlets make mistakes, sure. Sometimes big mistakes. There are blind spots. The financial underpinnings of news outlets can bend news coverage to the right or left, and gutted newsrooms employ too few journalists to churn out escalating demands for "content."

The hunt for eyeballs rewards contrasts, superficiality, and visuals. Television thrives on personalities who inject "analysis," which can be opinion more than reporting. Journalists write carefully for one news outlet while chatting more expansively under lucrative TV contracts for a second employer. Entertainment and news are a confusing stew.

"Fact-checking" used to be what reporters and editors did before publication and broadcast. Now it's also a political side dish, a reported presentation of point/counterpoint meant to serve a watchdog function. It also can backfire. The available evidence suggests the news media's assessments of fact only encourage people to dig in with greater confidence in their prior beliefs.

When the *New York Times* identified a Trump "lie" on its front page in 2016, before he captured the White House, was the headline a form of fact-checking, editorializing, analysis, or a gimmick?

Trump inspired heated debate in the journalism world about how to report on an administration with clarity and utility when a president persistently blames the media messenger to credit himself. "The media is—really, the word, I think one of the greatest of all the terms I've come up with—is fake," he said during a 2017 interview. Trump went on to complain that he received unfair coverage.

Today's tribal politics and splintered new-media environment are not the president's invention but, as a former reality-TV star and fixture of the tabloids, he certainly exploited what he found. Now he encourages his base to share his views, and they do. Researchers tell us that the president's strongest partisan supporters hold the news media in the lowest regard. Forty percent of Republicans who say they "strongly approve" of Trump's job performance also say journalists' ethics are "very low."

Yet it seems possible that, with the end of the Trump era, politics could calm a bit and presidential leadership may appear more conventional. Changes in the news business, on the other hand, are accelerating and are less foreseeable. Discouraging is the fact that public trust in the news media has fallen for a decade or more. On a brighter note: Americans say their trust in the news media can be restored.

ALEXIS SIMENDINGER is a national political correspondent with *The Hill*. She has covered five presidents, including President Trump, and reported for newspapers, magazines, digital outlets, newsletters, and a daily podcast.

WAS IT ALWAYS LIKE THIS?

QUINT FORGEY

HAVING ARRIVED IN WASHINGTON shortly after college at the beginning of 2018, I'd never covered a presidential administration—but I imagine very few in recent American history have proven as challenging and rewarding for a breaking-news reporter as Donald Trump's.

Although the breadth of coverage ranged from troop movements to turkey pardons, most of my writing on the news of the day revolved around the White House, tracking an erratic president who continued to dominate hour-by-hour media narratives even as he entered his fourth year in office.

With its careening storylines and abrupt proclamations by the president—some seemingly issued on a whim but almost always conveyed in a tweet—the Trump era made the journalist's charge to sketch the "first draft of history" feel all the more urgent.

The unpredictability of the president's online announcements, which could catch well-sourced White House reporters and even top Trump advisers by surprise, at times afforded me the opportunity to cover stories which might otherwise have been delegated earlier to more senior writers. And Trump's Twitter account regularly delivered news of major personnel changes, reactions to global affairs, and comments on domestic controversies that in past administrations would be transmitted to the media via more traditional channels.

The president's nonstop social-media use also made a few aspects of breaking-news coverage easier. Under previous White Houses, I assume I'd have sought comment from communications aides with more frequency. But Trump always served as his own chief spokesperson, and his tweeted statements were more unvarnished than what the West Wing press shop inevitably would have produced.

Of course, whatever advantages the president's singular brand of political messaging afforded reporters chronicling the administration on a breaking-news basis, its benefits accompanied similarly unconventional barriers Trump erected against press coverage of his White House.

Those obstacles, as well as the other manifold dilemmas Trump has posed reporters since 2015, are numerous and well-documented. And, while more experienced Washington journalists are better suited to judge their long-term consequences, I can speak to just a few of the difficulties that were inherent in daily Trump coverage.

Perhaps the most symbolic indicator of the administration's decayed relationship with the media came in the early months of 2019, when Trump's former press secretary Sarah Huckabee Sanders presided over what would be the last of the traditionally daily White House press briefings for more than a year. By then, they had become events separated by weeks.

Although some members of the media and critics of the White House had grown skeptical of the value of the televised sessions due to mounting concerns about Sanders's credibility, journalists henceforth were unable to question the president's top spokesperson in a formalized, semi-regular setting.

Instead, reporters seeking to probe the administration on the news of the day were forced to rely increasingly on Trump's impromptu comments at the end of White House events and his statements during bilateral news conferences with other world leaders.

Then there were the president's sporadic outdoor gaggles, conducted from the South Lawn as he prepared to board Marine One or after exiting the official aircraft. With the din of the chopper's engines obscuring journalists' shouted questions, those frenzied scrums also were problematic for news gathering.

Trump would pace freely before the throng of reporters, calling upon outlets at his discretion, and answering whichever queries he preferred. On some notably tough news days for the administration, the president bypassed the press altogether, ducking into his helicopter or beelining back across the grass to the White House.

When he did interact with the media or appear at official events, the president's proclivity for hyperbole and recurrent false claims also could hinder the efforts of breaking-news reporters who worked to quickly extract newsworthy statements—necessitating that journalists build clarifications or corrections into their stories to address Trump's inaccurate assertions.

The nature of the president's tangential speech pattern, too, presented complications when parsing his language. Trump tended to circle back to key themes in discursive responses to reporters' questions, alternately recasting a point more emphatically, softening a potentially news-making statement, or demurring with vague turns of phrase such as: "We'll see what happens." In covering a president contemplating consequential action or weighing in on an issue of international importance, it is incumbent upon journalists to capture these subtle shifts in rhetoric.

Reporters also faced other, less tangible dilemmas in the Trump era not directly engendered by the president himself but rather by his broader impression on daily news consumption. Chief among them was the constant struggle I experienced against becoming inured to the gravity of news events.

In an ever-spinning media environment marked by an excess of political bombshells from the White House, too many pieces of important journalism were lost in the chaos. Stories that typically would have commanded days of coverage in other administrations sometimes were minimized within hours of their publishing to dedicate precious column inches or space on digital platforms to the latest Trump-oriented revelation.

Amid this torrential pace of content, it was critical for journalists to contextualize the significance of certain episodes in Trump's presidency, even as they tended to blur together in our collective consciousness.

On some days, particularly when impressive feats of enterprise and investigatory work would fall victim to the barrage of Trump headlines, I was especially grateful to be a breaking-news scribe at this early stage of my career—crafting stories on deadline with a comparatively short shelf life. It was not an easy thing to see a more hard-won piece of reporting achieve less recognition than it might have in a calmer media ecosystem under a different administration.

One of the purest distillations of a related Trump-era media frustration came in the summer of 2017, after Donald Trump Jr. posted online his full e-mail correspondence documenting plans to arrange an audience with a Russian lawyer offering dirt on Hillary Clinton. Independent journalist Jared Yates Sexton, who long had been chasing the story of the infamous Trump Tower meeting, offered an instantly memorable, memeable lamentation: "I worked on this story for a year . . . and . . . he just . . . he tweeted it out."

There were other shared stressors among journalists who covered Trump, with most induced by the news cycle's ruthless pace. Washington reporters, already a workaholic bunch tuned in to the most obscure twists and turns of their beats, could have trouble ever fully disconnecting from a president whose fluid and far-reaching maneuvers required their attention.

Beyond the levels of engagement necessitated in recent years by social media, the news imperatives of the Trump era dictated that reporters simply no longer could afford to go offline.

Abstaining from Twitter for twenty-four hours over the weekend, for example, not only left me feeling woefully out of the loop; it diminished my ability to write quickly and competently in subsequent days on whichever news events transpired while I was unplugged. And, even in those moments of complete withdrawal at home, the intermittent buzzing of my phone alerting me to a new tweet by the president jolted me mentally back to the newsroom.

Every once in a while, a different kind of fatigue took hold when I returned to work, as the persistent themes of outrage and negativity that pervaded Trump's messaging could turn exhausting. Soon after starting on the breaking-news desk, I recall struggling to come up with new synonyms for the word "attack"—so often the optimum verb for the lead paragraphs of stories predicated on the president's remarks.

The sheer animosity of Trump's rhetoric regarding the media, which obviously did not color my coverage of the president, also was occasionally demoralizing for a journalist whose job was to constantly monitor and carefully report his commentary.

As I took stock of my first two years in Washington, I couldn't help but wonder: Was it always like this? Were the challenges of covering the Trump administration really all that different from the demands posed by those before it?

In casual conversations with journalists—and informal observations of my colleagues during the unrelenting series of news events generated by Trump's White House—I got the sense that there was a clear answer: for those who had covered previous presidents and then chronicled the Trump era, the job was even more merciless, decidedly draining and bizarre.

Being a relatively young reporter who had written only about President Trump, I hadn't benefited from enough experience to draw such contrasts for myself. Trump's Washington was all I knew, and I'm not yet sure whether my professional foundation in that unique political moment will enhance or distort my understanding of political journalism as I progress in my career.

I tend to think my experiences then—fielding time-sensitive stories with agility and competency in these hectic, historic news cycles—can only elevate my future coverage of a less volatile politics. Whether the incessant pace of news in the Trump era will slow down when someone else occupies the White House, however, is an open question.

After Trump eventually does depart office, or at least is unable to monopolize headlines in the way he has for the past half-decade, will the sheer volume of daily news engendered by his presidency leave with him? And will news consumers, who have become acclimated to a fever pitch of content over the course of the Trump era, allow it to abate under the next administration?

It remains unclear what exactly a post-Trump media landscape will look like, but I'm confident it will be characterized by the same diligence, doggedness, and integrity of reporting that proved paramount during his presidency—the type of coverage American journalism strove toward in the decades before his political ascendancy and will continue to achieve long after his exit from the national stage.

QUINT FORGEY is a breaking-news reporter for *Politico*. He is a graduate of Louisiana State University's Manship School of Mass Communication.

VII

TRUMP'S WORST HABIT

SARAH ISGUR MAINTAINS that Twitter brings out the worst of everyone: the worst of President Trump and the worst of the media. Both sides "have fully embraced the antagonism and cynicism of social media," she writes. Her background is unlike that of any other author in this book: she was the chief spokesperson for the Justice Department under former attorney general Jeff Sessions, and she now is a journalist.

THE VICIOUS, AND MALIGNANT, CYCLE OF TWITTER

SARAH ISGUR

IN 2013, PETER HAMBY published a piece with the Shorenstein Center at Harvard University entitled, "Did Twitter Kill the Boys on the Bus?" Riffing off the 1972 campaign memoir of Timothy Crouse, Hamby looked back at the 2012 presidential election and took to task what he saw as some of the excesses of a new breed of campaign reporters coming of age in the filter-free social-media universe who were turning the traditional rules of political journalism on their head.

In many ways, the Trump White House's relationship with the media was defined by the new rules Hamby saw emerging—"Instagram and Twitter-primed iPhones, an ever more youthful press corps . . . a journalistic reward structure in Washington that often prizes speed and scoops over context and thoughtful analysis, [and] campaigns . . . increasingly fearful of the reporters who cover them." Specifically, he cited Twitter's impact on these less-experienced journalists who tried to prove their bona fides with "the cynical tone of the online conversation and its preoccupation with insider gossip and process stories."

Eight years later, the media and the candidates they've covered fully have embraced the antagonism and cynicism of social media. But, for the first time, the White House was occupied by a president who appears to relish the gaffe-based media coverage that had become a focused fear for previous politicians and their political operatives.

These new rules were not created in 2016, nor was Trump the first president with an antagonistic relationship with the press. After all, even George Washington "expressed dismay" that his farewell address might not receive favorable attention from the press. A cursory study of the

Bush and Obama years reveals administrations from both parties increasingly cutting off meaningful access to reporters and finding their own ways to skip the media's filter to communicate directly to voters in response to what they would argue was an increasingly hostile press corps too focused on "gotcha journalism" that thrived on negative coverage.

In fact, it's as easy to see President Trump's surprise election as a response to some of these changing trends in journalism—often using journalists as a more reliable political foil on the campaign trail than his Democratic opposition. But it also is true that President Trump has embraced this negative relationship in a way previously unheard of, relishing the fights both legal and political that have come with revoking press credentials, canceling the press secretary's daily briefings, blocking critics on Twitter, skipping the White House Correspondents' Dinner, and calling out reporters by name at campaign rallies. Just to name a few.

If the political media, therefore, embraced new rules of engagement in the age of Trump, so too did the president. The result was a vicious cycle: a press corps that often has replaced skepticism with antagonism and an administration that takes advantage of that dynamic to erode the public's trust in the media. A lot of these internecine battles have played out on Twitter—a medium that rewards speed, snark, and strong opinions.

A few months into the Trump administration, the *New Republic* asked a handful of reporters about how Twitter affected their lives. Bret Stephens, an op-ed columnist for the *New York Times,* said Twitter was "the political pornography of our time: revealing but distorting, exciting but dulling, debasing to its users, and, well, ejaculatory. It's bad for the soul and, as Donald Trump proves daily, bad for the country." But, when asked what would happen if Twitter wasn't available, one editor said, "It would feel like a phantom limb," and another said, "We would all go into withdrawal."

While journalists may bemoan their Twitter addictions, they view it as a necessary one that often dictates what stories get told and who gets to tell them. "We tend to use Twitter as kind of an assignment desk," *New York Times* columnist Farhad Manjoo said in an interview with NPR. "If something is big on Twitter, we put it on cable news, we put it in the paper, we put it everywhere else." While some journalists could cut down on their Twitter usage, he added, "If you're a news reporter or just tied to the daily news cycle, you can't really ignore it," even though Twitter quips don't "work with the kind of higher calling of journalism to be thoughtful and nuanced and to report and to just kind of get a better and more comprehensive picture of the world."

Increasingly, the universe of frequent Twitter users that populates this reporter-heavy environment looks less and less like the American public. In its most recent study, Pew Research found that, of the fewer than 50 million US adults on Twitter, only 6 percent of those users account for 73 percent of tweets about national politics. That means fewer than 1 percent of Americans are frequently weighing in about politics on this platform. Not surprisingly, that tiny but vocal group tends to be the most ideologically polarized on both ends—with 55 percent identifying as "very liberal" or "very conservative." As of 2019, almost three out of four tweets about national politics are written by someone over the age of fifty (73 percent) or by someone who strongly disapproves of Trump (72 percent).

Overall, Twitter users in the United States are more likely to be young, college-educated, liberal, and wealthier. To look more closely at partisanship, 52 percent of US adults identify as Democrats or lean toward the Democratic Party, but far more than that—60 percent of Twitter users— say the same. The reverse is true for Republicans: 43 percent identify as or lean Republican, but only 35 percent of Twitter users do.

Journalists spending so much time on Twitter potentially can exacerbate the existing demographic bias within most newsrooms, in which 72 percent of Internet publishing or newspaper employees work in a county that Hillary Clinton won in 2016. Journalists also are more likely to live in counties with higher-than-average median incomes, to live on one of the two coasts, to be white, and to be male.

It's easy to see the double-edged sword that this highly polarized and demographically skewed online community can create. On the one hand, Twitter allows journalists to engage with and learn from one another, rely less on elite or official sources, and find previously untold stories that didn't make it to a traditional assignment desk.

But the consistency of opinions in the Twitter bubble also builds a false sense of coherence. In his seminal work on behavioral economics,

Thinking, Fast and Slow, Daniel Kahneman cites a study in which participants are given a legal scenario about a union field representative who was arrested for trespassing. After reading the scenario, some participants heard from lawyers from both sides and others heard only from one of the lawyers. The lawyers did not provide additional facts or relevant information; they only provided arguments based on the facts helpful to their own side. Not surprisingly, participants who heard only from one side were more likely to be swayed even though they knew they didn't hear from the other side. In fact, these one-sided participants "were more confident of their judgments than those who saw both sides." The point being, according to Kahneman, that "[i]t is the consistency of the information that matters for a good story, not its completeness."

The same scenario is playing out on Twitter every day. Journalists' ever-presence on Twitter can affect how reporters and their editors come to define what is "newsworthy" because the Twitter ecosphere amplifies this unrepresentative, highly polarized 1 percent of Americans.

In 2018, researchers studied Twitter's effect on how reporters view newsworthiness. They showed two hundred Twitter-using journalists "only headlines from the Associated Press website, while others were also randomly shown tweets that contained AP headlines but had been manipulated to look like anonymous tweets." The result was that "journalists who said they spend a lot of time on Twitter and rely on it for their work ranked the anonymous tweets as high or higher [in newsworthiness] than the AP stories." As the *Columbia Journalism Review* noted, the study showed that "journalists can get caught up in a kind of pack mentality in which a story is seen as important because other journalists on Twitter are talking about it, rather than because it is newsworthy."

Or worse, the anonymous, meme-heavy, and misleading bandwagon aspects of Twitter can distort reporting itself, *CJR* said: "A study of tweets posted by Russian agents working for the notorious 'troll farm' known as the Internet Research Agency found more than 30 news outlets—including NPR, The Washington Post, and BuzzFeed—had embedded tweets from fake accounts in their news stories."

Perhaps most damaging are the incentives that Twitter places on individual reporters. As newsrooms downsize, reporters are less and less likely to spend their careers at a single outlet. Building a brand becomes increasingly important to surviving in the industry. As Alecia Swasy, a journalism professor at Washington and Lee University, wrote, "[m]illennials have witnessed the massive downsizing of their newsrooms and view themselves as independent contractors who are in charge of their own marketing, much like corporate America curates their brands."

Twitter is unquestionably the easiest way for journalists to build their own following separate and apart from their employers. But the most obvious types of content that attract a large Twitter following—fast, digestible, snarky, opinionated—not only put pressure on journalists who are at odds with the values of a traditional newsroom but now may affect who decides to pursue a career in journalism. And, despite a plethora of social-media policies, editors and media executives still are struggling with how much control to exercise over their employees' Twitter voices.

For example, humor often is rewarded on Twitter—where a clever quip about a news item in 280 words or less can signal that the author knows the topic well enough to make a biting or sarcastic comment. The problem is that someone looking to build a following on Twitter then approaches every news item not from a place of journalistic curiosity but from the perspective of the next quip. As Manjoo put it, "because it is a kind of game where everyone's kind of competing to have the pithiest take on a thing, it affects our thinking. I noticed that I was thinking in Twitter quips, and that's not really that productive . . . [if] you're trying to produce good journalism."

Partisanship in an ideologically charged environment can work the same way. And one result is that otherwise non-opinion journalists can be found expressing strongly partisan opinions on Twitter. For example, John Harwood, who was at the time the chief Washington correspondent for CNBC, was the subject of scrutiny for tweeting this about the media's impeachment coverage: "hard for reporters to say plainly that the Republican Party, at this point in our history, is fundamentally broken but it is." He received almost 10,000 "likes" from some of his 350,000 followers.

Just over two months later, the president tweeted about Harwood, who by then had been hired by CNN, with the message to his supporters that reporting from journalists such as Harwood and networks such as

CNN should not be trusted, garnering 50,000 likes: "A so-called reporter named @JohnHarwood, who bombed so badly in the 2016 Presidential Debates that I thought he was going to be immediately fired (a Mini Mike type performance), is now with Fake News @CNN. A total loser."

It appears to be working. In a poll released during the impeachment inquiry, a majority of Americans believed that the media's coverage was biased. This follows longer-term trends as well. In fact, a recent study published by the *Columbia Journalism Review* found that the media are the top institution—even including the notoriously unpopular Congress—in which the American public has "hardly any confidence at all."

The president's attacks clearly were having an effect. As Pew found, "while Democrats' trust in many of these outlets has remained stable or in some cases increased since 2014, Republicans have become more alienated from some of them, widening an already substantial partisan gap." Not surprisingly, Pew reported "particularly notable increases in distrust of CNN, The New York Times and The Washington Post" among Republicans—all frequent targets of the president's attacks.

Unlike in decades past, voters have more and more choice when it comes to their media consumption. This requires media outlets to compete for an increasingly fractured audience. As Ezra Klein noted in his book *Why We're Polarized,* media outlets today cater to a smaller slice of the pie. In this new business environment, it didn't take long for someone to ask, "What if instead of telling people the things they need to know, we tell them what they want to know," he wrote, quoting a joke by MSNBC host Chris Hayes. From there, he argued, a new media rule emerged: "For political reporting, the principle is 'If it outrages, it leads.'"

The result is an American public that finds media sources that cater to their political identity and no longer has a shared trusted news source. "Republicans and Democrats place their trust in two nearly inverse news media environments," according to another Pew study.

Of course, if there is no shared news source that can be trusted by both sides, a president has the ability to influence which news sources his supporters look to and to ensure his supporters never even see the criticism from other sources.

But not everything about the age of Twitter journalism is bad. First, stories that may have been buried because of institutional bias or just bad judgment come to light for the very fact that journalists with their own brands no longer are beholden to a single news company. Ronan Farrow's reporting on Harvey Weinstein—which not only won him a Pulitzer Prize but arguably had a larger effect on American culture than any news story since Watergate—was allegedly killed when he initially brought it to his bosses at NBC. He eventually published his work with the *New Yorker.*

Second, transparency from reporters about their own biases and opinions may do more to encourage trust over the long term. If viewers have come to believe that every journalist has some bias, radical transparency actually can build credibility when those same reporters present facts to their audiences that are counter to the accepted narrative. Even so, for most journalists there should be some concern that sharing an opinion on Twitter makes them more likely to become invested in defending that opinion and the team that holds that opinion because it was stated publicly— a Heisenberg Principle of bias in which seeing the bias changes and increases the bias itself.

Last, the excesses of Twitter journalism need not last forever. After the current economic upheaval in journalism settles, traditional newsrooms may find they have an incentive to create social-media policies that require their employees to abide by the same editorial standards on Twitter—especially if the reporter is tweeting from an account verified because of the reporter's employment as a journalist.

SARAH ISGUR, formerly the top spokesperson for the Justice Department, writes for the *Dispatch* and is a CNN political analyst.

VIII

LOOK TO THE FUTURE

PETER BHATIA, president of the council that accredits journalism schools and sets standards for them, believes that those schools should do more with media literacy. "Many journalism schools have adopted some component of media literacy in their curricula, but it should be more overt, and more officially and formally stated," he writes.

HOW JOURNALISM
SCHOOLS CAN HELP

PETER BHATIA

IN JOURNALISM, we long have spoken of the love-hate relationships we have with our sources. The cops hate us, but they need us to let the public know they are keeping us safe. Athletes and coaches would be happy if we stayed out of their locker rooms, but they understand we help them speak directly to fans. Big developers, automakers, businesses of all sorts consider us a nuisance, but they know we help them sell products and make money.

And politicians, oh, they loathe us, but they get that a certain portion of the electorate still looks to the media—nationally and locally—to understand the issues and to shape opinions on officeholders and those running for office.

While the delivery of information has changed dramatically in the digital age, and today we are inundated with information and disinformation, we still hold the above truths to be self-evident.

No one has understood that better than Donald Trump. While he demonizes the media as the enemy of the American people (I proudly had T-shirts made for my newsroom staffs in Cincinnati and Detroit, crossing out "enemy" and replacing it with "eyes and ears"), he thrives on the nonstop stream of attention he received as a candidate and as president. He is without peer in creating spectacle, as many have written, and the media have dutifully followed that spectacle and, with little effective resistance, documented it, repeated it over and over and over, and allowed it to claim legitimacy with a willing segment of the public.

You can call Trump a demagogue with authoritarian tendencies, you can call him a serial liar—both are true—but he has manipulated the media and the public (despite heroic work by journalists at the *New York Times,* the *Washington Post,* and elsewhere) with an effectiveness that likely will damage our democracy for generations.

The slavish devotion to reporting his latest pronouncements—even when documenting falsehoods—has served his purpose of framing the press as evil and as out to get him—we're "terrible people," you know. The daily dump of tweets and falsehoods gets regurgitated dutifully by all the cable channels (and not just by his sycophants at Fox) and gives legitimacy to hate and poses a long-term threat to our fundamental freedoms, regardless of the occupant of the White House.

Here in the Midwest, the constant flaming from the Oval Office is more distant, but it would be foolish to dismiss it as without impact. There is, still, an appreciation for the role of journalism here, the shouts of "fake news" less common, and the relationships with sources more in the tradition of the opening paragraph above.

Journalists, at least those of us who labor in the mainstream, always have, locally and nationally, been devoted to accuracy and completeness, and checking and rechecking our work. In summer 2019, the *Detroit Free Press* published a groundbreaking investigative report documenting how Ford Motor Company had knowingly put cars on the road with faulty transmissions. Ford reacted with a fury and a campaign to denigrate the work that even included sending letters to journalism contests demeaning the reporting. In the end, the work stood up to the assault because it was meticulously documented and verified. The *Free Press* told the truth.

This sort of work is the heart of the journalism done every day in newsrooms that maintain essential traditional values of fairness and completeness. Fact-checking Trump falsehoods—a slice of the industry that has grown exponentially—is important. There is no doubt in my mind that 99.9 percent of so-called mainstream journalists retain their dedication to the truth.

But our world is more complicated and requires more dramatic action. I suggested during the early days of the Trump administration that the Washington press corps collectively should walk out when legitimate reporters are denied credentials or wrongly accused of supposedly bad actions. After all, scoops don't last more than a minute in the digital age, and isn't journalistic solidarity more important? That wasn't necessarily well received, and I could argue that my response was born as much of incredulity as it was reason.

But there's a larger principle at work. Doesn't our dedication to the truth suggest not reporting every nonsensical tweet or obviously inflammatory statement made at a rally? Memo to the morning shows: There's a lot of other news out there every day. Don't we have a responsibility to even more aggressively sort fact from fiction, even if in doing so we aren't stenographically reporting every word? Haven't we accepted that journalism today requires trying to understand what really matters to our audiences (in a serious way, not in pursuit of clickbait) and pursuing it with all the energy we can muster? Clearly, whether it is on cable news or on our websites, there is a need for what might be called in-the-moment fact-checking, a healthy skepticism toward false statements, and a total dedication to truth-telling.

Some might argue this is injecting opinion into our work, which the Trump propaganda has convinced a larger percentage of the public is what we do anyway. (This shouldn't be a surprise: We've always been accused of bias in our reporting. It's just gotten louder, more persistent and, sadly, potentially violent under Trump.)

While I have no illusion about changing the minds of my callers and e-mailers who suggest I should burn in hell—I prefer those who say they will pray for me—never has there been a time when it is more important to show our work.

I remember getting my son in trouble in fifth grade because I showed him how I calculate percentages, which was different from the way his teacher wanted. He got the right answer, but the process was not what was desired.

Journalists should show their process, explain what they did and how they got there. This isn't a new concept and is being widely adopted on newspaper websites. Here are the documents, here are the data, here's the interview transcript. Here's who did the story; here's their background. We show our work; the conclusion is inescapable. It's not a coincidence that many stories coming out of Washington these days include specific numbers of sources interviewed.

In the end, the process may not be beloved by all, but, if the answer is right, we show we are providing the truth. And we must be relentless in doing so, because we know those who twist it in pursuit of individual and partisan agendas will be equally relentless, as President Trump has taught us.

And, to help with this, some words of suggestion for our journalism schools across the country: For those who think journalism is dying, just look at journalism-school enrollment, the quality of young people coming out into our professions, and the impact they are having in newsrooms. It is impressive. These new journalists are smart, well trained and, of course, have been digital since the day they were born.

Every university student today should have training in media literacy. Students should be taught how to decode the ever-expanding media landscape, should understand how to sort a reliable news source from the latest troll, and should understand the importance of being a smart information consumer in this cluttered world.

Many journalism schools have adopted some component of media literacy in their curricula, but it should be more overt, and more officially and formally stated. It should also be part of student learning to develop that formal skepticism—not cynicism—that should inform reporting and news-gathering of all forms. Students should be taught to ask themselves, as a former colleague once said, to consider whether the opposite of what they believe to be true could be true. They should prosecute their reporting and prosecute their sources. They must be willing to investigate where information comes from.

This is hardly a new concept, but it is more needed today than ever. When they enter the field, students should be just as skilled at showing their work as professionals in the field.

The dilemma facing professional journalism today is real, serious, and urgent. The Trump phenomenon didn't end when he vacated the Oval Office. He has given voice to some of the worst instincts of Americans and has put in at least some jeopardy fundamental freedoms guaranteed by the First Amendment.

It's hard to imagine the First Amendment ever being repealed. One has to give some credit to the vast percentage of Americans who are fair-minded and willing to put the larger interests of the nation first.

But journalists and journalism must take larger responsibility for what Trump has created. We are not without blame. Sure, the growth of cable-news advocacy and the wild world of the Internet earn their share of the discussion, but there still is much that can be done. Engage with communities on more than a casual basis. Live inclusion. Make a place for all points of view. Initiate the engagement and inclusion; don't wait for it. Show our work. Explain how and why and what we do. And be relentless about it.

Many are practicing this already. But let's tighten up our definition of news. And, at every turn, be an advocate for truth.

PETER BHATIA is editor and vice president of the *Detroit Free Press* and serves as Michigan editor of the USA TODAY Network. He is in his fourth term as president of the Accrediting Council on Education in Journalism and Mass Communications, which accredits university journalism programs in the United States and internationally. Bhatia was the 2020 winner of the Benjamin C. Bradlee Editor of the Year Award from the National Press Foundation.

INDEX

CPSIA information can be obtained
at www.ICGtesting.com
Printed in the USA
LVHW032012250621
691162LV00005B/399